RISING ABOVE THE ROCK

LISA ABBOTT RICHARDS

Rising Above the Rock
Copyright © 2020 Lisa Abbott Richards. All rights reserved.

No part of this book may be reproduced, scanned, transmitted, or distributed in any form by any means, electronic or mechanical, including photocopying, recording, or by any information storage and retrieval system, without specific written permission from the publisher. The scanning, uploading, and distribution of this book via the Internet or via any other means without the permission of the publisher is illegal and punishable by law. Please purchase only authorized electronic editions, and do not participate in or encourage electronic piracy of copyrighted materials.

Please note that although this book is based on real-life and true stories, there are a few stories that have been fictionally dramatized for audience entertainment purposes only. The story is faithful to the author's experiences in the way that all creative non-fiction tries to recreate stories from memories as accurately as possible. The author has changed the characters' names to protect identities and privacy. Events, locations, and other details are assumed to be fictional. Nothing written should be assumed as an autobiography of the author's life.

Cover Photo Credit: Lisa Abbott Richards
Print & eBook Design: Dayna Linton • Day Agency • www.dayagency.com

ISBN: 978-1-7348421-1-1 (Paperback)
ISBN: 978-1-7348421-0-4 (eBook)

Library of Congress Number: Pending

Printed in the United States of America

10 9 8 7 6 5 4 3 2 1

RISING ABOVE THE ROCK

The brook would lose its song if the rocks were taken away.

— Elizabeth Kellogg

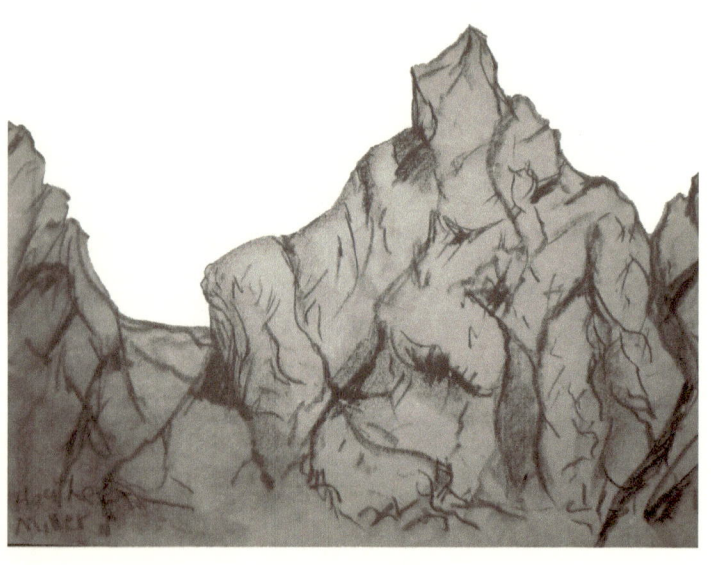

ACKNOWLEDGMENTS

I want to express my heartfelt gratitude to my Aunt Marilee, my friends Eva and Karen, and to my dear husband for proofreading my story so I could publish it. My husband also drove me around the valley, looking for the perfect spot to take the photograph of Mount Olympus. I also want to thank my friend Heather Miller for drawing the rugged mountain picture that you'll find to the left.

I feel deep love and gratitude to my Savior, Jesus Christ, for teaching me how to rise above my "rocks" and to live in thanksgiving daily.

I also wish to acknowledge all the friends and family who encouraged me to put this story into writing. You gave me courage.

Finally, I want to thank Dayna for helping me get my story out into the world. Hopefully, those who read it will receive strength and courage in their own trials.

To my dear family, you are my reason for living and overcoming. May you find the strength to fight and overcome your personal battles in life. Build something good with your own "rocks."

PROLOGUE

THIS BOOK IS A partial account of my journey of living, of laughing and crying, of loving and being loved more than I ever thought possible, of learning, of growing, of pain and joy, and of healing. Healing, in a physical way, in a mental way, in an emotional way, and in a spiritual way. This is also a deeper look into how we can rise above the "rocks" that we all encounter at different times in our lives. As I'm sure, many of you can also say, the "brook" that is my life has plenty of song. I continue to learn how to rise above and overcome each new rock that comes along. However, I have come to understand that each rock encountered needs to be handled or approached differently.

I do not like fanfare; I am not a public figure, nor are any of the other persons in this book. These are actual happenings in real peoples' lives, and therefore all names have been changed to protect their identities. Yet my message is the same for everyone, no matter your age, race, gender, background, experiences, or ethnicity: we *can* overcome any challenges (i.e., "rocks") that come into our existence. Though at times we cannot control who "throws" the rocks, or when, there are many other times that our personal choices actually gather or bring those rocks into our own world. The size of the rocks varies from day to day, week to week, month to month, and year to year. Sometimes even our Lord Jesus Christ will pick up a "rock," just to get our attention. You may recognize some of my "rocks" in your own lives. Please know that I do not wish to imply that all "rocks" are negative. Quite the contrary.

My hope in writing this book is to inspire or motivate each reader to turn to Christ for strength in traveling these rocky roads of our mortal existence, so that we can then rejoice in the fact that our "brooks" all have their beautiful song. Remember, "if God brings you to it, He *can and* will bring you through it." (~Anonymous, emphasis added.) I have learned that we have "rocks" only because God loves us and trusts that we can and will handle them well. I often think about the following poem that appears on the home page of the website PromiseofGod.com:

*If God had a refrigerator, your picture would be on it.
If He had a wallet, your photo would be in it.*

*He sends you flowers every spring.
He sends you a sunrise every morning.
And a sunset every evening.*

If God took vacations,
He'd take His with you.
He's with you every second of every day.

He wrote His songs just for you,
and created the birds to sing them.
Whenever you want to talk, He listens.
And He hears your every word.
He can live anywhere in the universe,
yet He chooses your heart.

Face it friend ...
He is crazy about you!

I dedicate this book to, and I reaffirm my love for, my family and friends. I hope you each know that you are my *everything*! If for some reason you don't know that, then I'm telling you again. Nothing is more important to me than my God, my family, and my true friends. For "no man is an island," as we were taught by the English poet and clergyman John Donne, 1572-1631. (Mr. Donne's complete quote is found at the following internet address: http://www.quotationspage.com/quote/29901.html.)

May you be uplifted at least a little by me sharing a small part of my story, and may you find renewed strength to face your daily battles. I hope we can all, "Be kinder than necessary, for everyone you meet is fighting some kind of battle." (~Attributed both to T.H. Thompson and John Watson.)

What a beautiful heavenly Gift is this earthly life! May you choose to live it with all the love, all the joy, and all the happiness God gives you, even through your trials.

Sincerely, your friend in Christ,

Lisa

Note: all scriptures quoted herein from the Bible are from the King James Version. There are also scriptures quoted from the *Book of Mormon* and the *Doctrine and Covenants* of the Church of Jesus Christ of Latter-Day Saints.

A new commandment I give unto you, That ye love one another; as I have loved you, that ye also love one another. (John 13:34)

CHAPTER 1

THE FIRST DAY AFTER

March 4, 1996

MY MOM, AGE 64, and widowed for nearly 24 years, rode the hospital elevator in silence up to my floor, lines of worry creasing her face. She had made the seventy-five minute drive from her home in Layton, Utah, to the hospital in Provo, feeling very pensive, her mind full of "what if" type thoughts. After all, she had no idea what to expect when she got to my room. Also, in times such as this, hospital elevators never move as fast as we would like them to move.

It was a crisp, yet beautiful Monday morning in March, and all Mom knew was that I had been seriously injured and that I was in the hospital, for probably a few days at least. Because of her worry over me, as though she wore blinders during her drive, she hadn't taken the usual time to really appreciate her favorite scenes of nature like the beautiful Rocky Mountains. Because she knew that there is usually a shortage of nursing staff in all hospitals, she wanted to hasten her drive. Mom had gotten a little medical training in years gone by through her employment, besides being a "nurse" to us five children over the years. So she determined that, besides just visiting, she must come to help care for me. Anyway, that's just what moms do.

Mom knew which floor I was on, but she didn't know where to find my room number, so she went to the nurses' station directly from the elevator. After being told where my room was, she walked down what I'm sure must have seemed to be the longest hallway ever known to man. The door to my room was partially open, and I was still under the influence of the anesthesia from surgery all night, so I was sleeping soundly—somewhat like a newborn baby sleeps immediately following a diaper change and feeding.

Unbeknownst to me, she pushed the door open farther, enough to allow her to step in and see me. I was lying on my back, with the head of the bed partially raised. My face was very bruised and swollen, so much to the point that she believed she was in the wrong hospital room. She spun on her heels and went quickly back to the nurses' desk, saying, "You must have made a mistake. That woman in there is not my daughter. Where is my daughter?" The nurse took her aside and very gently affirmed, "I assure you, there has been no mistake. The surgery she underwent all last night to stop the bleeding and to stabilize her wound area has made her tissues swell. If you would like me to walk with you back down there, I will." After contemplating her options, Mom said, "No, that's all right. I just didn't recognize her at all."

So Mom just sat there by my bedside watching me struggle for consciousness, coming in and out of the effects of the anesthesia. After what I think was about an hour, I finally woke up enough to realize that she was there, but smiling and talking would have to wait; I had already experienced more than enough pain for any given 24-hour period. Despite being hooked up to IVs for medication as well as for nourishment, the doctor had ordered that I should start trying to eat—but liquids only—as often as possible. Realizing it had been nearly 24 hours since my last meal, I agreed to try.

At first, Mom tried spooning the broth into my mouth. However, in dealing with what I termed "industrial strength" braces that were wired directly into my gums, I found that I had very little control over my oral functions. So after a couple of failed attempts to spoon-feed me, Mom asked the nurse if she could maybe have a dropper or a syringe to get the soup into me instead of on me. They soon brought her a few different types that she could use to gently squirt the "food" into my mouth. I was completely exhausted after consuming just two or three ounces, so I laid back to rest some more.

"Lisa, are you sure you don't want anymore? You didn't really take very much." I shook my head "no" ever so slightly and closed my eyes again, drifting into that ethereal realm where I didn't have to hurt while I was there. When you are in extreme pain, it's that realm you almost never want to leave. It has been said nothing hurts more than a burn. Well, maybe not, but I'd now discovered something that hurts at least as much as a burn.

I don't know how long I slept, but when I awakened later that day, Mom was still keeping vigil at my bedside. Then after a few more minutes had passed, I realized she had braided my long reddish-brown hair into very practical pigtails, so my hair wouldn't get all ratty and matted from laying in bed. The braids actually amused me slightly; so in spite of the pain, and in spite of the fact that I was 41 years old with four children of my own, I smiled as much as I could with my mouth full of stitches and metal, in gratitude for my mom's loving care, even when it came in the form of childlike pigtail braids. Mom had always had an attention to small details like that, and she and I both also knew that the nurses would never have the extra time to do anything with my hair.

Mom stayed the whole rest of the day, even though my 28-year-old younger sister Rachel was still at home alone. Rachel had a seizure disorder, so it was a little disconcerting for Mom to leave her alone for long periods of time. This made Mom's sacrifice to spend the entire day in my hospital room even more important to me.

I will not leave you comfortless: I will come to you. (John 14:18)

CHAPTER 2
MY YOUTH'S ROCK OF GIBRALTAR

June 13, 1972
Fairbanks, Alaska

I'D HAD A FAIRLY normal day at work. At age seventeen, I worked part-time as a sales clerk in a fabric shop just down the street from our home. The shop was owned by the wife of one of my dad's fellow police officers. This job was very interesting to me because I was learning how to sew, and I was fascinated with working in a shop that was a world of possibilities for what I might create. Though I only worked part-time at the shop, this particular day I had worked the whole day. I also worked part-time at the Carrington Company as a secretary for the parts department. I had just graduated from Lathrop High School three weeks before.

My alma mater was about 2,500 students strong, yet I was only one of approximately thirty kids in that high school who were members of The Church of Jesus Christ of Latter-Day Saints (sometimes abbreviated as LDS or

Mormon). So because of that ratio, we were a very tight-knit group. We were always doing things together, like monthly dances at our church, early morning gospel study classes before school (called Seminary), playing spoons in the school cafeteria—using the cafeteria's spoons—between our early morning youth Seminary classes and the time school started, along with youth group trips that we took at least once a year. Most of these other youth were fairly well known at our house because Mom and Dad had what I called a "Kool-aid house"—everybody always wanted to come over and spend time at our house because Mom was always baking cookies or bread, which she did with a now-rare expertise. And it didn't take very long for word to spread where to find goodies. When you're talking about the basic needs of teenagers, their number one need is usually to fill their stomachs.

So, I was just walking the few blocks home from work at the fabric shop and was at the corner by our house when I saw Dad leaving in his older pickup truck. It didn't matter that the truck was older; Dad was a very knowledgeable mechanic, and he had the engine purring like a contented kitty.

I had a strong and very close relationship with Daddy. We used to bicker about who would sit by him in church because, for example, he would take the digits 0-9 and draw them into funny faces to entertain us. I can remember—even after I started high school—that I would come home from school and sit on his lap in the recliner chair with my arms around his neck and his arms around my waist, while we waited for dinner to be ready, talking about how our day had been, at school for me and at work for him.

Daddy had three meetings that particular night, all related both to his job as a Fairbanks City police officer and to his affiliation in the local Veterans' group. When he saw me as he backed out of the driveway, he stopped and rolled down his window to greet me, even though he was in a bit of a hurry. "Hi honey, I've got these three meetings to go to, but then I'll be home, and I'll show you how to work this combination lock, which you asked for."

"Thanks, Daddy. See you when you get home. I love you." I reached up on my tiptoes to give Daddy a hug and a kiss through his truck window, and then I completed the remaining 1/4 block walk to our front door. I will forever be very glad that Daddy stopped for me, because as I've since learned, you just never know when it will be the last time you have a chance to say "I love you," or at least to show someone how you feel with a smile or a hug.

Therefore, I now believe we should always say our farewells as if it was our last chance to do so.

Later that evening, I was babysitting my three younger siblings while Mom and my older sister Tina went out power-walking. Looking back, it seems that Mom was always working on her health and fitness, having recruited Daddy at some point too, and she liked it better when she had someone to accompany her on her evening walks. That particular evening, Tina won out on the bid to go with Mom, so there I sat, watching TV halfheartedly. The younger kids were already in bed for the night, being ages 4-, 6-, and 8-years-old. Having just graduated from high school, I usually only had my work during the day and then relaxation or maybe youth group activities some evenings before bed.

Then came the first of two, now-despised, phone calls of that evening, just before the time I expected Mom and Tina to return from walking. It was from one of Dad's colleagues at the police department, asking for my mom. When I told him Mom had gone out walking but that she should be back in a few short minutes, he said, "Okay, I will try to call back in a few minutes." Remember, this was way before cell phones were invented, so I was pacing back and forth between the living room and the entryway where I could look up and down our street for any sign of Mom and Tina. I was feeling a little anxious because the caller had sounded to me like something was wrong.

When he called back a few minutes later, Mom and Tina were still not home, so he finally told me the problem. Daddy had suffered a couple of heart attacks and was being transported to the hospital. Mom later recounted that Daddy always carried these little tiny pills in his wallet, and he had told Mom that they were for his hiatal hernia. Mom had no reason to doubt his explanation, so she never questioned Dad regarding what were actually nitroglycerin pills for his heart.

The officer who called had told me that Dad had taken a pill after the first attack and then proceeded to his second of three meetings for the night. Soon after arriving at his second meeting, he took his second pill, but they weren't having the desired effect, and he was then taken to the hospital.

Following that second phone call, I was nearly beside myself, waiting for Mom to come home. Another fifteen to twenty minutes went by, and I practically raced out and met them at the foot of the driveway. Since 17-year-old girls don't usually have a lot of patience, and I was already consumed with worry, I had asked to trade places with Tina and go with Mom to the hospital while Tina stayed home and babysat. Mom told me to stay home while she and Tina rushed to the hospital. "So unfair," I grumbled to myself.

At least two hours went by without any word from Mom, and I finally decided to go downstairs to my bedroom. Probably thirty minutes after that, I heard the front door open and close. As I lay in my bed in the dark, still wide awake, I became alarmed when I heard their footsteps coming down toward my bedroom. I sat bolt upright in my bed as Mom opened my door very tenaciously and whispered, "Lisa, are you awake?" I said in my normal speaking voice, "Yeah, Mom, no way I could sleep until you came back home. How's Daddy?"

In reply, a sob tore from her throat, and Mom began to cry almost uncontrollably, making fear envelop my heart. "Dad's gone," Tina told me, while Mom collected herself enough to speak. "He died before we even got to the hospital. And I didn't even get to say goodbye!" Mom wailed. Then it was only a fraction of a second before the three of us were in a tight heap of tears and sorrow, rocking back and forth, hugging each other as we sat on the edge of my bed.

In the days that followed, as we prepared for Daddy's funeral, Mom would make random comments to us as she remembered them from her experiences at the hospital. One particular statement Mom made that I will never forget: "You know, Dad weighed fifteen pounds lighter that night than he had that morning. He must have had a huge spirit." Fifteen pounds? I've heard of a few ounces or maybe even a couple of pounds difference, but fifteen pounds? That's simply incredible. Years later, I came to realize that Mom knew exactly what Daddy weighed because in their bedroom, they had a very nice counterbalance scale like the doctors used, where they checked each other's weight every morning to make them accountable for the weight loss journey they were on together.

So my Rock of Gibraltar had left me, and I had absolutely no idea how, from that point on, I was going to handle work, college, or just everyday life. I wished I could turn the clock back to the day before and freeze time right there.

...my kindness shall not depart from thee, neither shall the covenant of my peace be removed, saith the LORD...

(Isaiah 54:10)

CHAPTER 3
A NEW BEGINNING

When we first moved to Alaska as a military family, we drove across the Alaskan border on my tenth birthday in September of 1964. This move followed my and Tina's adoption by Daddy, and our family being sealed for eternity in the Salt Lake Temple about two weeks before we arrived in Alaska.

That first winter, I remember walls of snow lining our front walk on both sides, from the street to our apartment's front door. Later, after we'd moved into our own home, I remember another winter where, for all the snow, no one could see the five-foot chain link fence which surrounded our yard.

One particular Saturday morning that winter, Mom woke up to the face of a baby moose looking at her through the kitchen window. She hurried to grab her camera to take snapshots through the window, wisely realizing that where there is a baby moose, somewhere close by, there is also the mother, whether you can see her or not. A neighbor, who apparently didn't have the same wisdom, came sauntering down the street with his camera around his neck. He never got a picture because the mama moose charged him almost immediately. He had gotten between her and her baby. The only reason he was able to get away was because he dived into a snowbank and buried himself, after he saw that he wouldn't be able to outrun her. Lucky for him, moose can't pick up the human scent through snow, and lucky that there was plenty of snow close by.

Life during the winters in Alaska is very beautiful but hard, at best, with the nuclear family still intact. When the Rock of the family passes away, it complicates things, to say the least. So despite the fact that Fairbanks was our home, and had been for nearly eight years, and because Tina and I would both be attending Brigham Young University in Provo, Utah starting the fall semester of 1972, Mom decided that she could not stay in Alaska with the three younger kids without having a man in the house. And winter would come in just three short months (September, not November or December).

Having then made the decision to move back to Utah, where she was born, Mom arranged to have Daddy buried in the military cemetery at Fort Douglas, Utah. We had the funeral in Fairbanks—actually in the military chapel at Ft. Wainwright just outside of Fairbanks—and then she flew with his casket down to Utah where the grave-side services were held so that Mom's siblings could be there to support her. We didn't know it at the time, but she and Daddy arranged for him to be buried double-deep so that her casket could be buried on top of his when that time came. That now seems like a very prudent idea for everyone.

Dad's funeral was attended by more people than I ever remember any other funeral service since. Right up to the time of his death, he had remained active in the Veterans of Foreign Wars (VFW) local chapter, the local Peace Officers' Association, and many other community service groups such as the Boy Scouts of America. We had to hold his funeral in the military chapel on the Army base because our local LDS chapel wasn't nearly large enough. In addition to the majority of our local LDS ward members in Fairbanks, we had the entire local Boy Scout troop, the entire Fairbanks Police Department, many members of the VFW group, and also many members of the local Peace Officers' group in attendance to bid him a final farewell. Interestingly, many of the people Daddy had cited and/or arrested during his tenure as a cop also attended.

You see, Daddy had made many lifelong friends in the Army during his twenty plus years of service, and he was also a very kind police officer. So when pulling someone over, i.e., for a minor traffic violation, Dad would always try to give them a "pep" talk about how they could avoid having a similar problem in the future. One night he had stopped a woman for running either a red light or a stop sign and was in the process of giving his "talk." All the while, she was acting very embarrassed and like she wished she could turn inside out or disappear, or something similar. When he had finished his "talk," he looked straight into her eyes and said, "Don't I know you from somewhere?" "Yes, you're my home teacher[1]!" she blurted. He had recognized her face, but because in his job, he saw so many different people on a daily basis, he had been unable to recall her name or where he knew her from.

---

[1] In The Church of Jesus Christ of Latter-Day Saints, every family has home teaching pairs assigned to them (now called ministering), to visit with them in their homes about once a month, give them a gospel message, and to be a neighborly-type of support if there are any problems or concerns requiring more assistance than the family can handle on their own. It's part of how we take care of each other in the Church.

Later that summer, having moved from Fairbanks, Alaska to Layton, Utah, with my two younger brothers and one younger sister, Mom settled into a new life where she could be close to her own brother and one of her three sisters. Tina and I proceeded to attend Brigham Young University (BYU), where I soon turned eighteen. But then Tina got married in August of 1973, so thereafter, I was left to find my own new friends on a campus of 25,000 students. I felt like I was suddenly lost in a sea of people, with no rocks to walk on and keep my head above water.

I majored in Music and minored in Dance while at BYU, but it should have been the reverse, because I found I did not have nearly enough educational background in Music to major in it, especially at such a large university. I also enjoyed the dancing much, much more than analyzing one piece after another of classical music for our Music class assignments. In fact, to this day, sometimes, I still use the nickname "Dancer." At one point, I even posted a little sign on my bedroom wall that read "I dance; therefore, I am."

Because of my great love for dancing, I auditioned for and was accepted to be on the Bronze team of the BYU Ballroom Dancers. My goal was to reach the Gold team, so I could travel around the world dancing. Now what is that phrase about the best-laid plans…

Truthfully, I spent my first college semester mostly playing, without much studying. I started out in an off-campus apartment with four of us roommates, and I eventually moved to another off-campus apartment where there were six of us. We all had different class schedules at different times, so the chaos was usually kept to a minimum. In addition, I discovered that all those times I had spent watching my mom make bread had rubbed off on me, and my roommates always loved it when I got the "baking bug."

One Saturday morning, I had baked a batch of bread and then left it to cool while I ran some errands. When I came back from my errands, I found that about half of the batch of bread was gone! Before I could accuse any of my roomies of pigging out on the bread, one of them came rushing out of her bedroom when she heard me come in. She began her explanation for the missing bread before I could open my mouth to say anything. It seems that unbeknownst to me, it was our apartment's turn to provide the bread for the Sacrament the next day in church. I had never been told anything about that, but I was secretly glad—after I got over the initial shock—that I had followed a spiritual prompting to bake bread that morning. This taught me that whenever I receive a prompting for anything, even to bake bread, I should do my best to following the prompting, whether I know the reason for it or not. Unfortunately, I have not always remembered that lesson since.

Most weekday mornings during my schooling at BYU, I had 7:00 A.M. dance practices, and sometimes while walking up the hill to the campus, I would be missing Daddy, and I would cry out and shake my fists toward the heavens, demanding to know why my Daddy had been taken from me. Then I had to wipe away the tears and pull myself back together before I got to class. I think when you're sleep deprived—as most college students are—your emotions are always closer to the surface than otherwise, so I was having a lot of emotional days. However, I also think that it is better to get your emotions out in some way than to hold them in and make yourself physically ill. I did plenty of expressing during that first year at college, which was also my first year away from home. I did find that every time I had one of my outbursts, even alone, the Savior was there for me, helping me feel the calm and peace I needed to function.

...contend no more against the Holy Ghost, but that ye receive it, and take upon you the name of Christ; that ye humble yourselves even to the dust, and worship God, in whatsoever place ye may be in, in spirit and in truth; and that ye live in thanksgiving daily, for the many mercies and blessings which he doth bestow upon you. (Alma 34:38)

CHAPTER 4
WELL ALONG THE ROCKY ROADS OF LIFE

A T SOME POINT, AFTER I had moved to a larger apartment off-campus, one of my five roommates had begun dating a very quiet guy who was a budding jeweler with quite a bit of promise for his future. I learned a short time later that my roommate was only halfheartedly dating this guy named Landon, and that she wasn't really interested in continuing to see him. Apparently, he had also expressed to her an interest in dating one of her roommates—me. (I guess when you're young, and without finesse, you take your opportunities wherever you can get them.) Because she wasn't really "into him," she told him that him dating me would be fine with her.

Well, long story short, after dating for several months, Landon and I were married in the Provo LDS Temple in May of 1975 when I was just 20 years old, and only 2½ years after I had begun attending BYU. So instead of a degree in Music or Dance, I ended up with my "MRS" degree, as everyone on campus would jokingly say. Upon my engagement, I then purchased fabric for around $50 (which was a huge purchase back then) and sewed my own wedding dress, which I still have in my closet today.

Landon and I found ourselves to be expectant parents right away, and four days short of nine months later, we welcomed our beautiful baby son Adam into our family.

I grew up not liking names to which parents or friends could add a "Y" to the end for a nickname, and I also wanted to avoid any "L" names for our baby because both mine and my husband's first names began with "L," as well as our last name. Additionally, I once knew a family that everyone's first names started with "J," and I remember being in some of the same classes with more than one of their children, where the teachers got so confused. My mom once knew of a family with the last name Peel, and they apparently thought it was clever to give fruit names to their kids (seriously?). As we were growing up, if Mom got upset at one of us, she would go through the whole list of us siblings before getting the right one. In Mom's senior years, she even added in the family cats' names. Landon and I didn't want to be inconsiderate in choosing the names our children would bear for their lifetimes because just growing up around other kids can be brutal enough sometimes.

Birthing Adam was a little hard on me because he was feet first in the womb instead of head down. I joke now that he tried to walk out into the world! Ultrasounds were not very routine back then, and his position in the birth canal wasn't discovered until I was already in full-on labor, which was too late to do anything about his position. So the doctor simply used forceps to deliver his perfect little head. Thank heavens, he only weighed 6½ pounds. I've heard "horror" stories from other women who had breech births, but I've never known of anyone else who had a double-footling breach birth like Adam's, though I'm sure they existed (and maybe they still do).

There was also a little bit of frustration mixed in with Adam's birth, too, because our "baby insurance" on which we had very faithfully paid the premiums for nine months declined to pay our medical bills in light of his arrival four days before his due date. We tried every avenue we could imagine to get the insurance company to pay, even going all the way to the Utah State Insurance Commissioner. He wrote a letter to the insurance company on our behalf, but they wouldn't budge. We had no idea how we would overcome this hump in our plans. It turned out to be the first of many stones in our pathway as a married couple. I also wholly recognize now that, in those days, our individual and joint skills for turning to prayer were still in the embryo stage.

At my postpartum checkup, my doctor discovered that I had an ovarian cyst on the left side. It was about the size of a medium orange, and my doctor wanted to "watch it" over the next few weeks. I remember thinking, no wonder I couldn't get my tummy to go flat after having my baby. No reason it shouldn't have, I told myself, because I was physically active and healthy; I was breastfeeding like they said I should because it was best for the baby, and because it would also help me get back to my pre-pregnant clothing size. Besides, it was just my first baby. Didn't every first-time mother have their tummies go flat soon after giving birth? Hah!

I knew of other new mothers who went home from the hospital wearing their skinny jeans, while I had to continue wearing my maternity clothes for a couple of months because nothing else would fit. I now find that I don't have time to associate with those skinny-jeans-types of women because I am a fitness professional (for more than 38 years), yet I never did get to wear jeans—let alone skinny jeans—home from the hospital after giving birth. Or maybe they don't really want to associate with me. Either way, we probably wouldn't understand each other very well.

So Adam was four months old when I was admitted to the hospital to have the ovarian cyst surgically removed. By then, the cyst had grown to the size of a three-month fetus. I actually looked pregnant again, because I am very short-waisted and only 5-foot 2¾-inches tall. (Sometimes I fudge a little and say that I am 5-foot 3-inches.)

I was still a nursing mom, and so the morning after my surgery, the first thing I asked for when I awoke was the breast pump. The nurse looked at me and exclaimed, "Oh, that explains your low-grade fever all night! We were worried that you were getting an infection following your surgery." That brief verbal interchange left me feeling like the nurses and doctors really should talk to each other more often. (Now that I have assisted a hearing-impaired nursing student complete her RN schooling, I realize that it was most likely a charting omission or error.)

Later that morning, my doctor was making his rounds, and he first went to the patient in the bed next to mine. (Only semi-private rooms were paid for by the insurance back then unless the doctor ordered otherwise for health reasons.) I didn't know it yet, but this other patient's reason for being in the hospital was that she'd had surgery to remove the endometriosis in her uterus. The doctor stated to her that she was doing well, but that the best thing for her to do would be to get pregnant as soon as possible. Since I couldn't help but overhear his advice to her, I sat in my bed, waiting for my turn with the doctor, silently fuming inside. After all, my baby was barely four months old. So when he came to my bedside, I looked at him square in the eyes and proclaimed, "I heard what you told her. If you're planning to tell me the same thing, I'll punch you right in the nose!" He laughed nervously and said, "No, no. It's two completely different situations. In fact, I'd rather you *didn't* get pregnant for a little while yet. We don't want to activate your ovaries too soon." I flopped back against my pillow with a huge sigh of relief. In the end, my post-surgical checkup that morning was quite positive.

Lead me in thy truth, and teach me: for thou art the God of my salvation; on thee do I wait all the day.

(Psalms 25:5)

CHAPTER 5
THE ROCKS BEGIN PILING UP

When Adam was only six months old, I was no longer able to make enough milk for him to be satisfied. After a few days of frustration in trying to feed my son, I called my doctor to make an appointment. At that appointment, he did an exam and then a pregnancy test. You guessed it; we were expecting again. I was stunned because I had thought that the breast-feeding would prevent me from becoming pregnant. When I voiced those beliefs to my doctor, he replied, "Oh my, no, there are no guarantees just because you're nursing. That only works for a small percentage of women." Now he tells me!

I remember going home that day from the doctor's office, where the pregnancy test had confirmed that I was indeed going to have a second baby. The drive home was one of very mixed feelings. I was very happy about the new life growing inside of me, but I was also a little stressed about the fact that this baby would be born so close to our first child and my subsequent post-partum surgery. As a result, I threatened heaven right out loud that, "If I have to have this baby so soon after my first one—and after everything else in between—it'd better be a girl!" Yeah, sure, like that would help anything. I hadn't yet learned the concept that I was not really in charge here. That lesson has been learned over and over again, as my life has progressed. I know now that I would have fared much better had I prayerfully sought the Lord's help to get through the pregnancy with good health and a proper attitude. There's a saying that if you want to hear God laugh, tell Him *your* plans.

Anyway, just fifteen months after Adam was born, I gave birth to our second son, Joshua. Josh finally came almost 2½ weeks past his due date (stubborn one, he was), and he weighed in at just under ten pounds! He absolutely filled the newborn clothing. I think at least three pounds of that weight must have been hair! It was literally laying on his neck as he was born, and as soon as they got him cleaned up, it curled right up, all over his cute "little" head. Because so many babies are born looking like cue balls, the hospital nursery nurses took advantage of the rare baby born with hair, and they had a great time brushing and styling his hair.

Because, in essence, I had twins that were fifteen months apart, Adam had developed the self-soothing behavior of sucking his thumb at nap time and bedtime, with one ear of a sock monkey that I'd made curled up in his little fist. He wore out about three sock monkeys by the ears before he finally grew out of them. Yet being the tradition-honoring person that I am, a few years ago, I revived the sock monkey presence in our family by giving Adam a sock monkey ornament that I found one Christmas; for another Christmas, I made him a Mr. and Mrs. Sock Monkey, complete with clothes that I crocheted. For Christmas of 2009, I found a giant sock monkey that stood about four feet tall, which of course, I proudly presented to Adam. And for Christmas of 2010, Adam returned the favor by giving me a purple sock monkey that he'd found in the store a few months before. He said he just couldn't resist (because purple is my favorite color); naturally, when he saw it from about 500 yards away while shopping with his wife, he made a beeline for it. Today the tradition is still ongoing.

Even now, though I'm wonderfully happy, it is good to think back on those moments that make me laugh or at least smile. I believe God gives us good memories to help keep us going when the going gets tough. Along with prayer and trying to honorably practice my faith daily, I have absolutely relied on those good memories. I still rely on them, because the going still gets tough more often than I would like. Now that I'm older and hopefully wiser, the "tough" is usually something which is out of my control, rather than a result of my own poor choices, with which perhaps you younger readers can identify. I now consider my happy memories as a kind of bridge over those troubled waters, or like those proverbial foot stones I could have used in my early days at BYU.

1: Therefore being justified by faith, we have peace with God through our Lord Jesus Christ:

2: By whom also we have access by faith into this grace wherein we stand, and rejoice in hope of the glory of God.

3: And not only so, *but we glory in tribulations also: knowing that tribulation worketh patience;*

4: *And patience, experience; and experience, hope:*

(emphasis added) (Romans 5:1-4)

CHAPTER 6
ANOTHER BEGINNING

MY MARRIAGE TO LANDON only lasted for about four years before I knew we were in trouble. I then sought the advice of an attorney—back in the day when they gave you a thirty-minute consultation for ten bucks—and decided that, since my efforts to get Landon to talk with me had been all but futile, and because our family also seemed to come last in his life, I didn't want to live this married-but-solo life any longer. The trust between us was gone, so I filed for a divorce. Our divorce was finalized in just four months (a rare occurrence these days, but then I also now believe it should be just as hard to get married as it is to get divorced. Maybe then people would think with their brains instead of their emotions before taking "the plunge." However, I don't believe in cohabitation either.)

RISING ABOVE THE ROCK

Apprehensively, I began my life as a single mom and soon found out it wasn't all it's cracked up to be. I did hold a very good full-time job with benefits, thank heavens, so I felt we would probably be okay no matter what. Yes, I had voluntarily placed myself in this situation (it being the lesser of two evils), but people whom I had previously believed were my friends quit talking to me all of a sudden. My home teachers quit coming to my home once a month as they had before, and people would get up and move after a few minutes if I sat by them at church. All this is behavior that in most circles is really considered to be quite rude, and certainly not very Christlike. I also began to question everything about myself and my life up to that point. It wasn't until later when I learned that questioning oneself during a major life change is pretty much the norm in human behavior. We just need to remember to invite God into the mix, so we don't get off track during our doubts.

Gradually, I built up a little more self-confidence after being shunned at church, and I began doing a few things like going out on dates or just going with some girlfriends from work to a dance club every so often. I still lived by my personal motto of "I dance; therefore, I am." So we friends usually had fun going dancing, and it was a great way to forget our troubles for that brief period of time.

I quickly discovered, however, that there are a lot of toads in the field of princes out there. Time after time, I would go home with at least a little disappointment in not being able to meet anyone suitable for me. I started joking with everyone that men are very much like parking spaces: all the good ones are taken, and the rest are either handicapped or way out there. Truthfully, though, I wasn't really kidding; I soon realized how really slim was the field of suitable, available men.

One night, I was at a dance club with just one other girlfriend, and she had met someone that she apparently wanted to spend more time with, so there I was sitting alone at a table to the side of the dance floor. Soon, this stunning blond guy with a great build approached me. "Hi, I'm Richard. I was noticing that you're actually pretty good out there on the dance floor, and I was wondering if you'd like to dance with me?" "Sure," I said, immediately perking up, "I'd love to." He whisked me away, and we quickly discovered that we both really enjoyed the type of dancing where you actually have to have a partner to do the dance. Now, this was in the mid- to late 1970s when Disco was all the rage, and in my humble opinion, there was never any better dance music written before or since. Today, I am in my mid-sixties, and I still really enjoy disco music, now mostly just teaching my water aerobics classes.

After that first night, when we met, Richard and I had several more dance dates, which eventually became dinner-dance dates. Then we started going to other functions together as well. At the time, he was not a fellow member of the Church of Jesus Christ of Latter-Day Saints, but that didn't seem to hinder him at all, even if what we attended was a church function. As for me, I was simply thrilled to have a great dance partner.

We discovered that Richard was five or so years younger than me, but that didn't matter because we got along very well together. We even met each other's families, and the fact that I already had two children did not seem to worry him at all in nurturing our new relationship. One weekend, I took my two boys to Eureka (the one in Utah) where Richard lived with his parents and younger sister. Thereafter, he and I grew so close and spent so much time together that we allowed our emotions to get the best of us one night. Even in the face of the love I was feeling in the moment, I felt strongly that I had to call my bishop the next morning to make an appointment with him. We are taught that confession is not only good for the soul but absolutely essential to our overall well-being.

On a side note, especially to all of you single ladies out there, I wish to pause my story here to give a very strong caution that I wish someone had given to me: please, please consider very carefully what could happen before you give in to your basic physical desires. With a prayer before each date, hopefully, you will be strengthened against doing anything that could be harmful to your self-esteem and to your future plans and dreams. Remember, you are a royal daughter of God; please don't let anyone treat you otherwise. God's plan for you is to save intimacy until after marriage. Remember to invite the Holy Spirit to go with you on all of your dates. Finally, don't stay out too late. That's when your natural defenses against error and sin are the lowest. Believe me, the Adversary takes full advantage of those moments if you don't take steps to shield yourself against him.

While the majority of today's world would think having two consenting adults become intimate was no big deal, I knew without a doubt that it was wrong for me to "partake" under those circumstances. I had made certain promises with the Lord (known as covenants in our church). So, not long after speaking with my bishop, I went through the resulting Church disciplinary council, which was unpleasant for me, to say the least, but still very necessary to set things right between me and my Savior.

I quickly realized that I was facing the consequences of my own personal choices in choosing some of those blasted shiny "rocks" that beckoned me. I have since come to know that shiny rocks are one of Satan's greatest tools. Even so, in the throes of my embarrassment and shame, I had determined to meet those consequences head-on and endure them well.

As a result, it was only a short time later that Richard and I were engaged to be married. He wanted to make an honest woman out of me, as the old-timers would say. In addition, two months before our wedding, Richard was baptized into the Church of Jesus Christ of Latter-Day Saints.

The fact that Richard had lived in Eureka, Utah all of his life, and still lived there at the time of our marriage, was the reason he was able to get a very good job with the Utah Department of Transportation right there in Eureka. It was a very stable job with great benefits because it was working for the Utah state government. Knowing this, and not wanting to ask him to give up his stable job after we were married (duh!), or worse yet, commute the hour each way from Provo-Orem where I was living, and for him to keep working in Eureka, we easily made the decision that we would move to Eureka as soon as we got married. We found a small house to rent and began our lives together in late March of 1980.

OUR DAUGHTER AMBER JOINED our family about thirteen months after we got married. Just one week before precious Amber was born, Richard had gotten consent from my ex-husband Landon to legally adopt Adam and Josh. So they officially became Richard's sons before Amber came into the world. In fact, on our way to the hospital in Provo, we stopped in Santaquin to pay off the adoption attorney—at my insistence. We also stopped at a drive-thru so I could get some ice chips, to stave off thirst during labor. I was reclined back in my seat, and the window attendant seeing my big belly, exclaimed "Oh, you look very close to your time!" To which Richard nearly shouted back, "She's in labor right now; would you please hurry?"

What else is a new father going to say? Beet red, she apologized and did indeed hurry.

Amber weighed just under 8½ pounds, with a beautiful face and hair, and she was very healthy. If I were to briefly summarize my life, I would have to say she was definitely among those top ten awesome blessings I've received in my life. Yes, I now do this type of positive mental reinforcement thinking all the time, but I haven't always.

Four years later, in June of 1985, right on her due date, I had our second beautiful daughter, Connie. The next day I had my tubes tied—because she came out a girl, and we were even: two boys, two girls. Besides, my body had endured four pregnancies, which were hard on me. I think I may have even been literally allergic to it. I was not a very gracious pregnant lady, nor did I enjoy pregnancy, which for me was nine months of morning sickness, the only relief coming after the birth. One year when I went to Amber's house to celebrate her thirty-something birthday, she said, "C'mon, Mom, you know today is your favorite day." I could only reply, "Well, maybe the day after!"

Sometimes out of the blue, I will think back on some cute little things my kids—and now my grandkids—have come out with. It always cheers me up immediately. For example, my boys used to wear blanket sleepers to bed when they were little because they could never keep their covers on. They must have been doing sleep Olympics in their beds or something. One morning, while Adam was new at the potty-going routine, I awoke to the sound of "Mommy, will you zip me down?" He just had to go, and he couldn't get out of his jammies!

Or the evening during my single-mom years that a house-mate of mine tried to teach Josh not to begin every word with the letter "H" (as was his habit). She chose the word "kitty" to work on with him. They sat on the top of the steps that went from my kitchen down to her private apartment, and she asked him to say "kitty," emphasizing the "k." Josh would obediently pronounce the "k" sound, followed by the rest of the word, "hitty." He was trying so hard. Over the course of fifteen to twenty minutes, their impromptu lesson evolved from him saying "ka-hitty" to "ka-itty" to him reverting back to saying "ka-hitty." I was quietly chuckling to myself, trying very hard to hide my laughter while cooking dinner, when she finally gave up. Josh actually overcame that language habit all on his own just a few months after that.

Then there's our precious, cancer-surviving young granddaughter, Diane, who would wrap her tiny arms around my neck, planting a kiss on my cheek and professing, "I lub you gwamah." Because Diane has so many different grandparents that she was trying to keep straight, she was talking to her mom (my daughter Connie) one day and said, "I want to call Purple Gwamah." Connie started laughing because she knew exactly who Diane was referring to—me. I've been accused of being obsessed by purple, but hey, I'm easy to shop for! That name has stuck for many years already, and now many other grandkids (and even friends) know me as Purple Grandma.

I also remember the words to one of my favorite songs by Ace of Base, "It's a Beautiful Life," that you should, "Take a walk in the park, hear a laughing child..." and with little effort, you can't help but recognize that it really is a *Beautiful Life*.

I have an acquaintance who self-assesses every morning as he awakes and says as long as the positives outweigh the negatives, he feels he's doing great. I've always believed that the most accurate answer to the question "How are you?" should be something like "Great; I woke up this morning, and I'm breathing air!" All the rest of life is manageable, "for with God nothing shall be impossible" (Luke 1:37).

Coming back to my story, let me back up just a little bit.

When Amber was still just a baby, Richard had taken on a part-time job picking cherries in season at a cherry plant about forty-five minutes' drive away from Eureka. We needed the extra funds because Richard's UDOT wages alone were insufficient to really support our family. I had always wanted to be a stay-at-home mom for my kids, but the reality of that was very short-lived. I had worked for most of my two sons' lives, and now it became apparent that I would have to go to work again.

Well, long story short, Richard had met some young "chick" at the cherry plant with whom he was becoming emotionally involved. Like him, she too was married, and she had a 13-month-old daughter. This threatened to rip our young family apart. So after a couple of very emotionally-trying weeks, I offered to let him go to school if he wanted while I worked. This seemed a reasonable solution to keeping our family together. Thus at that time, we moved to the Orem area (a return for me), and I took a job at Provo Canyon Boys' School while Richard went to a local trade-tech school to become an electronic technician. Orem is like a sister city to Provo.

When Richard graduated as a full-fledged electronic technician, we then moved to Magna as first-time homeowners. Magna is a township in the westernmost side of the Salt Lake Valley. Though it's a township, it's still much larger than Eureka. We both got jobs at Sperry Univac (which shortly changed its name to just "Sperry" and then later to "Unisys"). Things began going fairly well, even though we'd made so many recent changes in our lives. We'd been able to get into our first home through a special government financing program, and I thought we had a pretty good life. I *thought*.

Truly my soul waiteth upon God: from him cometh my salvation.

He only is my rock and my salvation; he is my defence; I shall not be greatly moved. (Psalms 62:1-2)

CHAPTER 7
STONES OF MOUNTING PROPORTIONS

EVEN THOUGH I KNEW I had been 100 percent faithful, Richard had accused me that Connie was not his. It wasn't until much later that I realized this should have been a red flag to me. I had proved him blatantly wrong just by the mere fact that, even from birth, Connie bears such a strong physical resemblance to her father. I was strongly motivated to make this marriage work because my first marriage had ended after only four years when I had discovered only a few of Landon's many secrets. I was yet to learn of Richard's secrets.

OUR FAMILY HAD GONE camping over the Labor Day weekend of 1986, in a remote area southwest of Eureka, Utah. It was actually Labor Day morning, and we were breaking camp to return home. Thinking only to prevent forest fires, we buried our campfire with dirt and began folding up the tent and putting away food, chairs, dishes, etc. About thirty minutes into our packing, Connie, aged fifteen months, was toddling around camp when she tripped over a *rock*, a stick, or a dent in the ground, and fell hands first into the fire pit, where the buried coals had been smoldering for the last half hour, getting hotter and hotter. Her right hand was more near the center, but both hands were severely burned. Gratefully, Adam happened to be close to her right then and snatched her up. We flooded her hands with the water in the jug that was already packed away in the trunk of one of our cars. Since we didn't own a vehicle large enough to hold our whole family plus camping equipment, Richard stayed behind in our Subaru to finish packing up camp. I grabbed Adam holding Connie in the back seat of my Malibu while I "flew" back to Eureka to get help. He had one of his hands on her binky, and the other was holding the chemical ice pack around her hands. He would alternate the ice pack with the binky, one until she cried with pain, then the other till she cried with pain.

I tried three of Richard's relatives living in Eureka before I finally found somebody home, his Aunt Fiona. She got a bowl of ice water and a towel, called her EMT daughter across the street, who then drove us to the nearest hospital in Santaquin, almost forty-five minutes away. I then held Connie with the towel and the ice water, plunging her towel-wrapped hands into the ice water until she cried, then removed them until she cried. We left word for Richard to meet us at the hospital, and away we went. I was in shock by then, but I didn't give in because I had to take care of my baby daughter.

Richard made excellent time meeting us at the hospital ER, where the doctor then performed the first of what I was to learn would be many debridements. (This is a process wherein the dead, burned skin is scrubbed off the wound, exposing the raw tissue underneath—excruciatingly painful.) They gave Connie a sedative before this treatment so she would sleep through it. Then the doctor told me I couldn't be in there during said debridement, even though I was very insistent not to leave my baby. He also said that I should relax because, "This wasn't the worst thing that's ever happened to a child." I sobbed, "But it is to any of my kids!" I don't remember who, but two people had to physically pull me into the waiting room because I had started charging that unfeeling ER doctor. I was going for his throat after what he'd said to me about my baby.

Following that first treatment, the ER doctor determined that Connie needed to be at the Burn Trauma Unit of the University of Utah Medical Center, a 2½ hour drive from Santaquin. He called ahead so they would be expecting me, made sure that Connie had enough sedative to last for that long drive, and I proceeded to take her there while Richard took the other three kids home to Magna and arranged for their care by a neighbor.

I was met in the ER at the U of U hospital by a burn trauma team, where they proceeded to do another debridement. Of course, this awakened her. They had parked me on a stool next to the exam table and were trying to teach me how to do debridements at home. Just a few minutes into this second treatment, one of the techs looked up at me, saw me looking like a ghost, and said, "Are you okay?" By this time, I was crying, hard, and all I could do was shake my head. He immediately removed me to a chair with it's back against the wall. When I managed to murmur that I am hypoglycemic and had not eaten since breakfast (it was then mid-afternoon), he raced to get me some juice. This brought me back only partway to reality. I was still in shock, and my blood sugar had long since crashed for lack of food.

At that point, the team had sort of slowed their frenzy to care for my daughter, had given her another sedative, and asked me if I could handle doing these treatments at home—*four times a day!* Again, I could only shake my head, eventually saying I just needed food and rest. They made instant arrangements to keep her overnight.

After they had given me more juice and some crackers to sustain me long enough to get home, I kissed my sleeping Connie on the forehead and left her, with me crying all the while. I'd only gotten a brief glimpse of what was to come in the next months ahead.

As it turned out, we had four nurses living in our ward/neighborhood, who were able to arrange their schedules so they could alternate coming to our home four times a day to assist either Richard or me in the debridement and dressing change process. Connie quickly learned that a trip into the bathroom with any one of those four nurses at our home meant pain, and she began to cry before we even began the treatment. Each treatment caused her to scream with her whole soul, and to bleed profusely all down both arms while we scrubbed the dead skin from both hands. It was so exhausting for me to have to put my baby daughter through such pain that I soon only had the strength to make it from one dressing change to the next.

At the time of Connie's burn accident, Richard was working swing shift, and I only had 24-hours of emergency leave left at my job. So we determined that if I took two hours off at the end of every workday, I would be home in time for him to go to work. He would manage the first two dressing changes of the day, and I would manage the second two. Looking back, I wholeheartedly thank God for those four nurses and their willingness to help us. We could not have accomplished this grave task without them.

Five days after Connie's burn accident, my grandmother died. We buried her on my birthday three days later. While at the funeral home, I asked my sister Tina to assist me with one of Connie's needed debridements. We went into the restroom of the funeral home, and Tina began to cry when she saw all that I had to make Connie endure four times a day. I understood her shock and tears.

Following twelve days of this horrendous debridement routine, the burn trauma team finally determined that Connie was ready for hospitalization and skin grafts. It took two skin graft surgeries and eleven more days in the hospital for them to complete her initial treatment. By then, I was out of all leave from work, so Richard would visit her before he left for work, and I would race up to the hospital immediately after work to be with her. After school, our other three children were in the care of neighbors again. Forever, I deeply thank God for those neighbors.

During the time before Connie's surgeries, each of my other three kids systematically hurt themselves (albeit minor injuries), to the point that when I got that third panicky phone call at work saying somebody had slammed their hands in the bathroom window, I was so stressed out, I said, "Is there bleeding?"

"No, but I can't get them to stop crying."

"Well, if anybody else gets hurt, so help me, I'll come home and finish the job!"

"*Mom!?!*" For which I then had to apologize, tell them I really did love them, and then take a quick break at work so I could go cry/pray in the restroom. Always the Savior comforted me when I would ask for His help.

What followed Connie's hospital stay was months and months of stretch therapy several times a day, in between which she had to wear special gloves called Jobst gloves, to put pressure on her burn scars as they healed so they would be minimized. The doctors also instructed us to be faithful with her stretch therapy, so she would have the highest possible function of her hands. I would sit in my rocker with her on my lap, and I would sing while rocking her, carefully stretching and holding each finger. This is also a very painful process, and she would finally reach her limit, crying, "Mommy, no more, no more, no more."

Then she would fall asleep for a few hours, and I would collapse. I would plead with Heavenly Father to let me take her pain. Every day was like this.

By this point, I was taking time off from work without pay, and we were just barely scraping by with our finances. I didn't realize it at the time, but Richard was withdrawing emotionally more and more as the weeks and months passed. I gradually began to feel that married-but-solo feeling all over again.

Regarding the woman taken in adultery:

...he lifted up himself, and said unto them, He that is without sin among you, let him first cast a stone at her. And again he stooped down, and wrote on the ground.

And they which heard it, *being convicted by their own conscience, went out one by one*...(John 8:7 - 9)

(emphasis added)

CHAPTER 8
ON THE EDGE OF A ROCKY PRECIPICE

In early 1987, Connie became ill and dehydrated, and she ended up hospitalized with pneumonia. When we were able to take her home from the hospital, I had to do a sort of tapping therapy on her back with a special hand mallet that they sent home from the hospital. This tapping was to keep the phlegm in her lungs loose and moving, and it was especially important to do on her before letting her sleep all night. One evening it was after dinner, and everybody had bathed and finished homework, and I was performing the tapping therapy on Connie prior to putting her down for the night. About 9:30 p.m., there came a knock on the door (who in the world?) Richard was still working swing shift till about midnight, so I asked Adam to answer the door. It was a representative from the local Division of Child and Family Services (DCFS), there to inspect my home! Supposedly my boys were sleeping on an old couch in an unfinished basement. It was really a double sized hide-a-bed in a room behind the attached garage of our tri-level home. And yes, the room was unfinished, but we had the windows covered with sheets, there were rugs on the floor, with electricity and heat being plentiful in the room. The DCFS rep conducted the home inspection while I finished Connie's tapping therapy for the night, though I had to try really hard not to cry. Thankfully, he came back to the living room and stated that he didn't understand what anyone had to complain about, that my home was cleaner than his own. He said he couldn't tell me who had called in a report about our home, but he left saying there was no problem there. Since it was called in by someone who had obviously been inside most (if not all) areas of my home, I had my suspicions about who had called; yet I've always wondered why? What could they have possibly gained by doing that to me?

Subsequently, I started seeing odd charges on the phone bill, and Richard tried to explain them away by saying he had purchased gifts for me that were not correctly delivered, so he called to report them. That sounded pretty fishy to me, and I later learned that they were calls made to "services" that would talk sexy to you—for a price per minute.

About a month later, I was supposed to sing a song in church for the Relief Society ladies' meeting. So I got in the shower first. Then Richard went to shower. With only one bathroom in our home, we all had to take turns. While Richard was in the shower, I was dressing for church in our bedroom. I went to my dresser to put on a watch and some earrings, when I found a three-page handwritten letter from Richard, confessing to me all the things he had done.

And all saints who remember to keep and do these sayings, walking in obedience to the commandments, shall receive health in their navel and marrow to their bones;

And shall find wisdom and great treasures of knowledge, even hidden treasures;

And I, the Lord, give unto them a promise, that the destroying angel shall pass by them, as the children of Israel, and not slay them. Amen.

(Doctrine & Covenants (D&C) 89:18-21)

CHAPTER 9
A MAJOR ROCKSLIDE, WITH AFTERSHOCKS

THINKING BACK, MY FIRST divorce had left me feeling stone-cold about close, intimate relationships, rather than feeling bathed in rock-solid security.

My separation from Richard took place in late June 1988, after his many insincere apologies, promises to do better, and then more disagreements or even arguments between us. Our divorce was finalized in October.

Richard had shown unwillingness to emotionally re-engage and help our marriage, so I was now on my own again, a single mother; this time with four children to finish raising. I was grateful to God every day for my very stable job at Unisys of more than five years, and my great family health insurance coverage that was included. I also continued being very active in church callings, and I was trying to do everything that was expected of me—not only in church, but also at work, and with my kids. It's probably a good thing I was only in my thirties because today, in my sixties I wouldn't have the physical or mental energy to undertake the monumental task of being a single mom of four. God's life plan for all of us is definitely age-appropriate.

I HAD WAITED PROBABLY about six months following my second divorce before even allowing the thought of going out on dates to take hold in my mind. I had gone dancing several Wednesdays at a local dance club in downtown Salt Lake City and had met a few guys who wanted to take me out. But my heart still felt somewhat closed, like there was a stone covering its entrance that needed to be rolled away, so up to this point, I had responded to them all that I only wanted to dance, and please leave it at that.

There was, during this same period of time, a seemingly very nice older, yet very attractive gentleman at work, thirteen years my senior and yet young at heart, who was showing an interest in me. At that time, my best friend Sandy was his secretary, so that's how I met Donald. Eventually, Donald even escorted me to a company dinner that was held for his department. I guess you could say that it was our first date, and we had talked for a few hours during and afterward, getting to know each other a little better.

Subsequently, since Donald was in a position of higher authority than I was at the company, and since his department had available overtime hours, I began to take on more work hours to better manage the financial needs of my family. The major drawback of working this overtime was that I was rarely home to spend time with my kids, and they were often left to their own devices for too many hours after school each day. In hindsight, if I could go back and change that decision, I wouldn't have worked so much. It was not the most important thing at that time—my kids were—and it surely wasn't worth all the misery that followed.

Donald and I also began spending a lot more time together, both at work and after work, when it wasn't "too late" at night. Sometimes we would run away from work for a "long" lunch break, and since he was my boss at that time, it wasn't a problem. He also got me into writing poetry, which I found was a very satisfactory method of expressing my innermost feelings. My whole world suddenly became a source of lyrical thoughts, both funny and serious in nature. My poetic ventures continue to this day.

I eventually completed my assignment on Donald's team at work, so I continued to work in my regular office with no more overtime, and he and I then dated very steadily, but only on his terms. He traveled a lot, which he told me was for his work, and there were some times that he was just not available. I remember that he had laid down some "rules" in our relationship: things such as I was not to go dancing without him, even if he was out of town; I was never to call his home phone; neither of us would see other people socially; he would only be available at certain times, and the list goes on. Those of you who have ever been involved in a controlling relationship are probably breaking out in a sweat at this point, remembering your own mistreatment. I now know that these "rules" should have been red flags to me, but I truly believed that I had grown to love Donald, so I didn't really think about how much he was controlling me. I now realize I overlooked a lot because I felt I had a genuine love interest.

Life went smoothly—in general terms—until one day in May about 2½ years after my divorce from Richard. I went into work as usual and was settling into my routine for the day when my boss called me into his office. A couple of weeks prior, the employee rumor mill had said that the company would be laying off approximately ten percent of its workforce, so we were all on pins and needles at work, and the tension in the air was so thick you could have cut it with a knife. We saw various office signs such as "The floggings will continue until morale improves;" or a picture of fish in a blender with a caption that read "I can't stand the tension!" Unfortunately for me and my kids, my boss told me I was to pack up my personal belongings and leave by noon that day.

In a whirlwind of emotions, I did as I was instructed. I had lost much: seven-plus years of seniority, my paid vacation time, my paid sick leave, my steady income, our family medical insurance, a place to teach aerobics (a newly acquired favorite activity), and some of my dignity that day, as I tearfully said my goodbyes to my friends and left the building for the last time. Strangely, Donald didn't seem that surprised or even upset about my layoff. To this day, I've wondered if he had something to do with my name being put on the shortlist. I don't worry about it anymore, because I know I can't change the past. You can't do anything about the past, but you can do *everything* about your future.

Being worry-free is an attitude we would all do well to strive for before hard times hit. Just think to yourself, if something is upsetting to you, will it matter in five minutes? If so, how about in five days? Five months? Five years? In all of eternity? In other words, is it really worth fretting over? I have on my bedroom mirror a little poem by LeGrand Richards that I usually try to remember: "For every worry under the sun, there is a remedy or there is none. If there be one, hurry and find it; if there be none, never mind it." This has helped me over and over throughout my adult years of life.

Of course, my nearly daily exercise, now having taught aerobics for more than 38 years, and now also teaching yoga for more than four years, has only further boosted my positive outlook. So if you're not already involved, I recommend that you find some type of exercise which you will enjoy. I can promise that you will definitely like the boost of attitude you get from exercise.

...all these things shall give thee experience, and shall be for thy good.

(D&C 122:7)

CHAPTER 10
GLIMMERS OF HOPE

DESPITE BEING NEWLY OUT of work, I had planned for and promised my kids a vacation to Disneyland late that summer. Before the layoff, I had acquired a Discover card with a $3,000 limit; plus, I had been saving a little money. So after a little bit of careful planning, I rented a minivan (because no vehicle I owned could have fit us all or made the trip safely), and away we went early one morning in August of 1990. Thankfully, Adam and Josh were both old enough to help me drive the twelve hours from Utah to California. To save money, we stayed in a motel within walking distance of Disneyland, and we also bought a disposable cooler with some breakfast and lunch food, going out only for dinners. We had a blast at Disneyland for three days; then, Adam had to fly back home for work. We spent another full day at Knottsberry Farm, and then Josh had to fly back home for work also. The girls and I spent our last day in California at the Hollywood Wax Museum and took pictures of each other standing next to our favorite wax figure. We bought fun tee-shirts that had a picture of our head photo-shopped onto a model-type body. The caption read, "Look what happened to me in California." I don't know about my girls, but I still have my shirt. It brings back great memories, along with our picture of all of us on Splash Mountain. It was a little hard for me to put each of my boys on a plane by themselves, and it was also a little scary for them because it was the first time flying for both of them. Plus, I was now solely responsible for the twelve-hour drive home.

To break up the return drive, I had previously arranged to stop at the home of an Alaskan friend of mine to stay the night and catch up. Gina and her husband David had been married since shortly after high school graduation, and they had bought property in Sandy Valley, Nevada. They had lived in a trailer house while they built their home very slowly, only as they could afford the materials. So when they moved in, they had no window panes yet, but they also had no mortgage payments. What a grand idea! It would take a lot of planning and even more self-discipline, but doing that would certainly alleviate many of life's stressors if we could all find a way to be that patient. I really wish I had thought of home-building like that.

Anyway, it was fun to meet her kids and have her meet two of mine and to stay up late catching up a little bit from the many years we had not seen each other.

Four months following our trip to Disneyland, I found a secretarial job for a small company in West Valley City. My boss was a very masculine woman who also seemed to have a Little Napoleon complex (even though it's usually males who manifest that). On an almost daily basis, she would say things like, "How many times do I have to tell you I'm in charge?" After just a couple of months of working there, I could tell my skills were very unappreciated. I was not allowed to think for myself at all in completing tasks for this woman. I felt it wasn't going to work out. Then one day, I was called into her office and given thirty days to find another job and get out.

During this era, besides working full-time, I attended night school to learn the trade of court reporting. I was thoroughly enjoying school, being mentally stimulated and even physically challenged to learn the theory of court reporting, while practicing to simultaneously build more and more speed on my steno machine. It took me eight months to get through theory, and typically a student is writing at fifty words per minute upon graduating from theory. To become a nationally certified court reporter, one must write at 225 words per minute with 95 percent accuracy. Quite a ways to go after finishing theory! But I felt I had finally found my niche in this world; I definitely wanted to make this my career.

I spent that evening in school after being given thirty days to leave my still fairly-new job, but I was seething and worried. *It is a full-time job to hunt for a job*, I thought to myself. *How will I ever be able to find openings and go to interviews if I'm still working?* With a prayer in my heart and determination to ultimately succeed in reaching my goals, I finished that evening in school at the usual time of 10:00 P.M. But instead of going directly home, I drove to my office building. I packed up my few personal belongings, filled out one final time card, wrote a brief note of goodbye to my boss, and left my office key on her desk. "I need to take control over my life again," I said out loud as I rode the elevator down to the first floor and walked to my car.

Having been let go once again, I knew that I needed help. My home teacher at the time, Harry—who was also a Salt Lake County sheriff—had suggested that I needed to apply for unemployment. This was a foreign concept to me because I had never even considered doing that before. To me, it was like getting money I had not earned.

But Harry assured me that I had earned it by working all those years, yet not ever drawing from it. "Besides," he said, "you are still honestly seeking real employment. In the meantime, you need to take care of your kids and keep a roof over your heads, don't you?" I nodded and agreed to start the process the following morning.

I completed all the necessary paperwork to start receiving unemployment compensation, but I soon learned that my former boss was contesting my application. Her basic claim was that I had not fulfilled my employment duties and that I didn't "deserve" this compensation. I was struck with the fear that she might succeed in blocking my survival efforts, so I talked to Donald about it one evening while we were out together. He suggested that I sit down as soon as possible before the scheduled hearing to make a log of every event or occurrence related to my work at that job, along with gathering the backup documentation. Donald even went to the hearing with me for a little moral support.

I was nervous but found that the hearing officer was very kind and allowed me to "testify" first on my own behalf. Thanks to Donald's suggestions, I was able to easily answer all the hearing officer's questions with the proper backup documentation. Then it was my ex-boss's turn.

With each question he posed to her, she spluttered and flailed through her paperwork, which was not organized in any fashion. Ultimately, she claimed that I was not giving her 100% of my time while at work (what human being can do that?), and that I wasn't worth the $15/hour wages she had paid me, and that's why she "invited" me to leave. Even though I probably shouldn't have, at that point, I interjected that my pay was on a monthly basis, not hourly.

The hearing officer had listened to her "testimony" and was growing ever more impatient with her. I was feeling much more confident with my case by then when finally the officer asked her one final question: was I hired as an hourly employee, or was the job advertised as a monthly salary? She hesitated but finally admitted it was monthly. Good for her, because if needed, I still had my copy of her newspaper ad in my stash of documentation. With that, the hearing officer abruptly ended the hearing, saying that there was absolutely no reason that I should not be receiving this compensation, and she was summarily dismissed from his office. After she left, I stretched my hand toward the hearing officer. With tears of gratitude beginning to well up, I shook his hand and thanked him for his thorough consideration. Then Donald and I left quietly to celebrate.

What I really wanted to do was squeal out loud in delight and dance a jig (but I knew that would be inappropriate there).

AT SCHOOL THAT YEAR in about October, we students all received a flyer about a national essay contest for court reporting students, the ten grand prizes being a brand new electronic-write-to-a-floppy-disk type steno machine, valued at $4,000; something I could only dream about owning. Donald suggested that I make my essay a poem so it would stand out in the crowd. I liked that idea, and I began writing down some thoughts on the assigned topic of "Court Reporting and Its Value to the Judicial System." I entitled my poem "Word Photography"©, and once I had it finalized to my satisfaction, I submitted it with butterflies in my stomach. Then I kind of forgot all about it after a month or so.

One January day, I was at home practicing my steno machine writing speed while my kids were away at school. I was still unemployed but trying to give my schoolwork as much attention as possible while I wasn't working. My phone rang unexpectedly, and the lady on the other end gave me her name and said she was calling from Stenograph Corporation. My heart nearly stopped when she announced to me that I was one of the ten national winners of the essay contest,[2] and what color did I want my machine to be? I could hardly breathe, almost laughing and crying simultaneously. She gave me the color choices, and while I was disappointed not to have purple be one of the choices, I chose a burgundy machine instead of gray, green, or blue. She told me congratulations again and then hung up. I wanted to tell the world, but I was home all alone! I called Donald at work, and he seemed pleased, but not really excited for me. Wow, I had hoped for a lot more from him than that.

Of course, I celebrated with my kids when they got home from school that afternoon, but they didn't really get what all this meant to me, because they were just kids, after all. Though somehow, I couldn't wipe the smile off of my face knowing that I was now the proud owner of a nicer steno machine than the owner of our school, who was a seasoned court reporter herself.

---

[2] You may read my winning poem in its entirety at the end of this book.

O that there were such an heart in them, that they would fear me, and keep all my commandments always, that it might be well with them, and with their children for ever!

(Deuteronomy 5:29)

CHAPTER 11
A BOMB AND ITS FALLOUT

SOMETHING I'M VERY PROUD of: I wasn't on unemployment very long because I had worked a few jobs here and there as a temporary, or until I found something better where I was happier or more satisfied. Then just more than a year after my "Little Napoleon" boss, I finally landed a great job at Evans and Sutherland (E&S) in Salt Lake City. Also, before I had been laid off at Unisys, I took on a part-time job as a night/weekend cashier at a Rainbo gas station not far from my house. That lasted for about 2½ years—phew—and remember that I was working full-time during the day, teaching aerobics after work, and still going to night school. But you "gotta do what you gotta do." So far, I had managed to make my house payments and keep my kids in the same house, same neighborhood, and same schools, so they wouldn't have to leave their friends. I felt pretty darn good about accomplishing at least that, because I knew the alternative would have been living in some rented dumpy apartment somewhere that was probably some kind of pest-infested. Or worse yet, I could have ended up homeless with the risk of DCFS taking my kids away from me.

At E&S, I was one of two secretaries for the very large International Business Group, which I thoroughly enjoyed because there was great variety to my job. Additionally, I was gifted with many international trinkets as the guys would return from a business trip to their assigned countries.

Shortly after I started working at E&S, I began teaching some aerobic classes onsite, too, because they had a place where people could work out but no structured classes. I've long since learned that motivation stays higher if there is a schedule of classes for people to attend. I was helping the employees, but I also once again got the benefit of working out regularly as well. However, for these classes, the only pay I received was having the company media guys volunteer to make a beta videotape master of each of the three different kinds of classes I was teaching there (low impact aerobics, step aerobics, and toning/sculpting). I was given the master videos, and I still have them today, but I have transferred them to DVD. And it's kind of nice to work out in my own home sometimes and kick my own backside with my own videos of me teaching. (How many people can say that?) Since that was now more than 25-years-ago, I can still have that goal to work toward. (Yes, I've gained a little weight over the years, but if you don't know already, you'll learn it happens to most people as we age.)

Early 1993

As usually happens with large companies like E&S, when the economy slumps, the company immediately downsizes its workforce. So after 2½ years there, I was laid off. By that time, I was the senior of the two secretaries in the department, and I was making more money than the other gal. They usually don't look at who has been there the longest; instead, they eliminate the most amount of money in wages.

My relationship with Donald had continued for more than six years by that time, and so he helped me drive my stuff home the day I was laid off from E&S. On the way home, we stopped at a Wendy's to get a shake and to talk, because I was understandably upset about losing yet another great full-time job. While we sat sipping our shakes, he said, "I just wanna get married. How about June?" I was a little shocked, to say the least because he had never mentioned marriage to me before. Since I thought I was in love with the guy, I agreed it was time.

So he drove his car with some of my stuff and I had the rest of it (not just my personal office stuff, but all the steps and other equipment for the aerobics classes, too). When we arrived at my house (incidentally the one and only time he ever came to my home), he sat down with my kids for a few minutes and told them, "Your mother and I are in love, so we're going to get married in June." My girls, of course, were excited as most young girls are about that sort of thing. My boys seemed to be a little more wary; naturally, I thought, since they had already been through two of my marriages and divorces.

Despite my plans to marry Donald in another six months, I continued to look for another full-time job somewhere in the valley. He called me out of the blue one day and told me about a company where his son's girlfriend had just quit and that I should apply there. So I did. They hired me within a week or so of my having been laid off at E&S.

I was hired as the Rotary Division Secretary for a drilling company, and I settled into my new office with the usual photographs, etc., that we all use to personalize our workspaces. Part of my responsibilities were to relieve the front desk switchboard operator for her lunches and breaks. That was fine with me; the more variety at work, the better. Most of the rest of the employees were a little stand-offish to me, but I wasn't there for social reasons, so I just concentrated on my work and didn't think much about it.

One morning, after I had worked there for about two months, I received an interoffice e-mail from the front desk receptionist inviting me to join the girls for lunch. It seemed very out of character for them, but I thought maybe they were finally starting to warm up to me. We all drove in the same car to the restaurant they had chosen. Conversation on the drive seemed a little strained, but I pushed that thought from my mind and tried to think positively. We all got seated at our table, and we had placed our orders, when the receptionist suddenly looked at me with tears welling in her eyes (she was pregnant, so I thought it was hormones) and she blurted, "Lisa, I don't know how best to say this..."

"Just spit it out Sally; whatever it is, it can't be that bad." Yet in my mind I was asking, *Or is it?* So she took a deep breath and almost wailed, "Donald is married!" My eyes flew wide open, and I instantly felt totally "ganged up on" and speechless. All I could say was, "Oh-h-kay." That was apparently the wrong response because she then demanded, "Well, did you know???" I felt as though I had been sucker-punched in the stomach by a gigantic bodyguard or something.

"No, I certainly didn't know. He told me he was divorced. He even gave me "divorce papers." Why else would I be walking around work saying we were getting married in June? And by the way, how do you know this?" So then I began to understand why the rest of the office gals were there. It seems that the day before this luncheon "date," Donald's son and "girlfriend" came by the office to show off their new baby. They were, in fact, actually married, and Lana was actually Donald's daughter-in-law. It turns out that the reason she had quit working there was to have her baby. Well, I was assigned to cover the switchboard upfront when they came to the office that day with their baby. They had come in the back door because she had worked there for years and everyone knew her, and her husband, Matt. My desk was near the back door, and of course, I had a picture of me and Donald arm-in-arm posted on the wall next to my desk. Matt immediately recognized his father in the picture and reportedly said, "Why is my dad's picture up here, and who is that woman he's with?"

So, the proverbial "fan" was now—well, you know. I mustered the courage to thank the office gals for being willing to tell me this horrible news, and we went back to the office and had what proved to be a very difficult afternoon for me. I did the best I could, but needless to say, I was very embarrassed to be working there, knowing that practically the whole rest of the company knew about my situation by then.

After work, I went to night school but couldn't concentrate very well, so I went dancing for a while to burn off some steam. Then I went home and started ripping down pictures off my walls and discarding knickknacks from my shelves. Though it was now late at night, Adam was home but still on the phone with one of his friends, and he continued to talk/listen on the phone while he watched me for a minute. When I finished in the living room, I practically ran upstairs to my bedroom and started purging my walls and shelves in there. Adam could tell I was very upset about something (or someone), and he hurriedly ended his phone call. He bounded up the stairs to my room and said, "Mom, what the heck are you doing?" All I could think to say was, "It seems Mr. Peters is married!"

"No way!" Adam exclaimed. "Yes, way," I replied as I continued to remove trinkets and pictures from my room, throwing them into a huge box, not caring if they got broken. "What are ya gonna do, Mom?" So I looked at him through my tears and shook my head and started to sob. I knew what I had to do; I just didn't want to do it because it was going be hard, and it was going to hurt my heart and soul.

At this time, Donald was away on a business trip, and I was supposed to pick him up at the airport in two days. That didn't give me very much time. Since my relationship with Donald had become intimate more than 5½ years before, I knew I had to call my bishop and confess. But first I wanted to call my stake president (a Church leader with higher authority), because he was an attorney, and I wanted to show him the so-called "divorce papers" that Donald had given me.

So I made an appointment for the afternoon of the day Donald was to return from his trip. For two hours, I sat in my stake president's office, telling him my story, crying, and having him make phone calls to check on the facts. They all were proven true by the persons on the other end of the phone calls. In those two hours, I learned that not only was Donald married, but he was also a member of his bishopric! Immediately, his stake president began turning the wheels of Church justice for Donald, and my stake president set into motion the Church disciplinary procedures for me. You see, I was a current temple recommend holder at that time, and so was Donald, which meant we had both lied in our recommend interviews. God is a merciful God, but He is also a just God, and these actions by Donald and myself could not be ignored.

I knew all along that I would have to take my own "lumps" for my wrong and bad choices during that whole six years. In reality, having it out in the open was quite a relief, even though the hard times for me were just beginning all over again. No human being can keep a secret for very long without it eating them from the inside out. There is an oft-quoted saying by Mark Twain that I believe applies very well to keeping secrets: *"Anger* (or secrets and lies) *is an acid that can do more harm to the vessel in which it is stored than to anything on which it is poured."*

I was ultimately let go from my position at the drilling company, because Donald's family simply could not leave me alone at work, calling and blaming me for all the trouble they were having in their family, apparently unwilling to accept the fact that he could have done something so horrible as to date me voluntarily, knowing full well he was married.

So, Donald flew home on schedule, but I wasn't at the airport to meet him as we had agreed before he left, and when he called, I refused to answer my phone. Let him make his own way home from the airport; I was too busy rearranging my life—and I was still furious with him for lying to me for more than six years. I was furious with myself for being so gullible that he had actually succeeded in those lies for so long. As Abraham Lincoln taught us, *"No man has a good enough memory to be a successful liar."* Yes, Donald's gig with me was finally up.

Counsel with the Lord in all thy doings, and he will direct thee for good; yea, when thou liest down at night lie down unto the Lord, that he may watch over you in your sleep; and when thou risest in the morning let thy heart be full of thanks unto God; and if ye do these things, ye shall be lifted up at the last day. (Alma 37:37)

CHAPTER 12
THE ROCK

THE NEXT TWO AND a half years saw me picking up the pieces of my life and then rearranging the puzzle of my soul once again. I was still determined to succeed, but the scars were now so much deeper than ever before, and they were going to take a lot more time to heal. Even though I didn't yet know how I would do it, I absolutely knew I would survive!

As you may have already guessed if you know any details about the Church of Jesus Christ of Latter-Day Saints, because this was the second time in my life where I'd lived in such blatant disregard for the covenants I had made—and even for the Ten Commandments—I was ultimately excommunicated from membership in my church after the whole six-year fiasco of my life that was Donald.

I now refer to him as "Stupid" on the rare occasion that the subject comes up because I so resented him for all the misery he had brought upon me through his lies, and I resented myself for going along with the unmarried intimacy of our relationship that I knew was wrong and against my promises and my covenants to God.

No one can live happily ever after in a negative environment or with a negative mindset, so I knew I must get over myself and start working to repair the damage I had done to my relationship with my Savior and my Heavenly Father.

I began participating in the LDS adult singles group that was active in the Salt Lake Valley, attending parties and firesides and hikes, etc., with the group. At one particular fireside I attended, the speaker was the owner of a men's clothing store here in Utah, but more importantly, he was the father of a man who was killed by one of Mark Hofmann's bombs.[3] While I don't remember Brother Christensen's exact words at the fireside, I will never forget his message: always stay in focus with the Lord at the helm of your life, and keep control over your own actions; above all, make it your goal to work on keeping the Ten Commandments every single day of your life.

Following the fireside, I remember that I went out to my car and pounded on the steering wheel, crying out, "Donald, you just weren't worth it! Get thee behind me,

---

[3] You may remember that Mark Hofmann is now in the Utah State Prison for murder and forgery of many supposed LDS historical documents, among other crimes.

Satan!" I vowed from that day forward to never give anyone or anything that much control over my life again, save the Lord only. A vow we might all do very well to make and keep.

At these single adult activities, I had met a couple of guys with whom I dated several times, and we always had a lot of fun. One guy I dated was only a distraction for the time being. Kent was very nice and treated me well, but I knew from the beginning that it wasn't going to go anywhere. We were just too different. That was probably also because I had received a prompting from the Spirit that Kent was not "the one" for me.

Then there was Ned, about whom I was feeling and thinking more seriously. His wife had died some years before, and he totally blamed himself for letting it happen, even though she died in her sleep from over-medicating herself. (Talk about baggage!) So after a few months of dating me, he got scared that he was dishonoring his dead wife's memory and just walked out of my life one day.

Sometime later, I learned Ned had taken a work transfer up to the Seattle area. All of a sudden, Ned wrote me a letter bemoaning the fact that he was up there alone and that he had let me go. *C'est la vie*, I thought to myself. It was his loss. I told him that I had become engaged by then, but that I wished him every one of God's blessings. He eventually got married again, but he's never really sounded as happy as I am in my current marriage. I used to keep in touch with these guys and their wives at least once a year by sending out Christmas cards, but that was the extent of it, really.

To DIGRESS A LITTLE bit, besides dating, since dancing was still an inherent part of my very being, I continued to dance every Wednesday night down at the Bay, mostly with my newly-acquired dance partner Alex. He was such a breath of fresh air from my daily troubles and so much fun to dance with. We started getting to know each other a lot better, even going dancing together on nights other than Wednesday and in other places than the Bay, although the Bay was our favorite place.

One night at the Bay, I knew things had made a shift in Alex's mind. We had been dancing for a couple of hours already when we went downstairs to the other dance floor for a different genre of music, where they happened to be playing slow music right then. After that slow dance, before letting me out of his arms, Alex looked me in the eyes without saying a word and then suddenly kissed me. I was quite taken aback but realized instantly that I'd enjoyed it because I'd kissed him back. Alex was always making me laugh, and he treated me like gold. Though I wasn't about to end our dance partnership, I began to wonder where this could possibly lead, because Alex was not LDS or even religious. After all my failed relationships, I knew I didn't really want to get serious with a person outside my faith.

Yes, I was still temporarily outside the membership of my own church at that time, and they may have briefly taken the girl out of the church, but nobody would ever be able to take the church out of the girl. I think I may have started putting up rock walls around my heart that very night.

Alex and I continued dancing together in the weeks and months thereafter, and there was more kissing and hugging intermingled with the dancing. A few weeks after Christmas of 1995, he invited me to go with him for a weekend in the spring to enjoy Utah's Arches National Park. The idea was very appealing to me because I had not been able to vacation at all since Disneyland with my kids five years before. My boys were old enough now to tend the girls for a couple of days, so I told Alex I would work on the arrangements at home, but that I would love to go with him.

We settled all the plans and picked the weekend we were going to go and began looking forward to our adventure together. When Friday, March 1, 1996, rolled around and it came time for us to leave, I assured my kids I would be home Sunday evening, and I told them where I was staying. We had a wonderful weekend together looking at all the beautiful things Mother Nature had to offer us in the Moab area. I was even inspired to write another poem when we got to Dead Horse Point because the scenery was so breathtaking.

That Sunday morning, we packed up to leave, ate a lazy breakfast at a restaurant in Moab and got into Alex's car to drive home. It was going to be about a four or five hour car trip, but we weren't really in a hurry. We didn't really want the fun to end, and the weekend had gone fast enough as it was.

Alex and I both loved Disco music, and so, of course, we had quite a stock of it to play in the car during our trip. We had stopped for lunch somewhere along the way and were again heading homeward. It was beginning to be late afternoon-early evening, and we were driving along talking, laughing, and singing the songs together.

Our conversations covered a full gamut of subjects, including that Alex was beginning to have very strong feelings for me. I teased him that if he didn't want to fall in love with a "Mormon" girl (like he always joked about with me), he'd better hurry before I got re-baptized because that was definitely on my agenda. We had just concluded a conversation about near-death experiences, which ended by Alex telling me he didn't think he really believed in those things that so many people had written about. I told him that I definitely believed, but I couldn't speak to the specifics of anything because I had never experienced near death that I could remember.

The song we had just finished listening to was one of our very favorites, "Your Love" by Lime. (If you love Disco like me, you should look it up and get it. Great stuff. The video's a little weird, but the music is awesome.) Alex and I both knew all the words, so of course, we were singing along. The shadows of an almost setting sun were playing different shapes on the mountainsides as we drove through the canyon. It was so beautiful, and I was feeling very happy.

Without warning, I suddenly found myself in a kind of bright, but almost misty place, where there was a great inner and outer warmth and a lot of light and so much love. I realized there were other people around me, and we were all communicating, but there were no words being exchanged. I felt a very strong impression, even a command, that I *must* go back, even though I didn't know where I was or how I had gotten there. And go back to where? Home? But where were my kids, and why weren't they with me? I never left my kids alone for very long at any time, did I? I realized much later that Alex wasn't even part of my thoughts while I was there—wherever *there* was.

Then again, without warning, I was moving very quickly, like I was flying/floating/soaring through a gray, lifeless, tunnel-like area. At last, I woke up, felt the pain, heard the panic in Alex's voice, saw the hole in the windshield, the rock on the console, and all the blood gushing from my mouth. What on earth had just happened?

Alex had stopped the car and ran around to my side to grab his brick-sized cellphone[4] from under my seat to call 911. He also grabbed my gray plaid jacket from the back seat so I could hold it over my mouth as a compress.

---

[4] It was only 1996, and personal cell phones were still a rather new invention back then.

He was crying nearly hysterically while he was trying to connect with the EMT's on the phone, but we were still about two miles up the canyon when this—what?—had happened, so his cellphone kept cutting off. He raced back to the driver's seat and hurriedly drove the final distance to the mouth of the canyon, and finally was able to maintain the phone connection. He gave them our exact location, now at the mouth of Spanish Fork Canyon, and less than thirty seconds after he hung up, they were at our car.

The ambulance personnel at once began preparing me for transport to the nearest hospital in Santaquin, Utah, just a few minutes away. Meanwhile, I had finally managed to stop crying, and all I could feel in my mouth, besides the excruciating pain, was several loose teeth and a thick, warm liquid (probably blood). I just kept thinking, *Don't swallow your loose teeth; just keep them moist in your mouth, and they'll be able to put them all back.* Oh, and the blood just wouldn't stop.

The next thing I knew, I was in the ambulance strapped to one of their gurneys with a cold pack on my mouth. They must have given me some kind of shot because I was now starting to feel drowsy, and the pain seemed like only a dull ache. I couldn't really see anything except the ceiling in the ambulance, but off to my side, I heard Alex repeatedly saying, "Where is she? Where is she?" Then I felt the paramedic take my hand and place it into Alex's hand to finish the ambulance trip. But why was Alex in the ambulance too? Was he badly hurt as well?

O all ye that are spared because ye were more righteous than they, will ye not now return unto me, and repent of your sins, and be converted, that I may heal you? (3 Nephi 9:13)

CHAPTER 13
NOT JUST A BOULDER

THE "WHAT" THAT HAD happened was that as we were driving through the canyon that night of March 3rd, some kids riding in the bed of a pickup truck were horsing around and had thrown a rock about half a brick in size toward our car going the opposite direction. Physics laws demanded that it would come sailing through the windshield and hit me in the mouth because I was sitting directly in its forced path. Physically, I received a through-and-through laceration to my upper lip, my maxilla (upper jaw) was completely shattered and dislodged from place, five teeth were permanently knocked out, and my hard palate was split zigzag all the way back to my soft palate. My teeth couldn't be saved because there was no foundation in which to put them back, just gaping holes of broken jaw bone.

The non-physical effects of the Rock in my life would take years to manifest and overcome.

One of the first things I remember doing when I was in the ER at Santaquin was motioning that I wanted a writing utensil and some paper. The kindly nurse then brought me a clipboard and a pen. I scrawled "Want LDS blessing." She knew exactly what I meant because it is very common for LDS priesthood holders to be present in Utah hospitals just for the purpose of administering to the sick. She had them there at my side within fifteen minutes.

Before the Elders (priesthood-holding LDS missionaries) got there to pronounce a blessing of healing upon me, I requested a mirror from the nurse. She looked at my penned request and replied, "Oh no, you don't want to see; trust me." I quickly wrote on the paper that yes, I did want to see, so that I would have a reference point for my journey of healing. Since the injuries were to my mouth and face, I knew it would change my countenance; I simply wanted to know how much of a change I was dealing with. I was quite shocked when she finally handed me the mirror, and upon seeing my battered reflection, I began to cry almost instantly. Just then, the Elders walked in, so I quickly pulled myself back together in their presence.

Another thing I wanted was for Alex to call home and tell my kids what had happened. As it turned out, he was transported in my same ambulance because he had glass sprayed in both eyes when the rock hit. He said he saw it coming, but in that split-second, he had literally no time to react. He was treated and released, having shed enough tears to cleanse his own eyes of nearly all the glass. Later I thought about that and realized he had driven approximately two miles to the mouth of the canyon with glass in both of his eyes. Wow.

At that point, Adam was 19-years-old and had his own vehicle, so he called a neighbor to take 10-year-old Connie for the night, and he drove Josh and Amber down to the hospital. They got there within about forty-five minutes. I don't even want to know how fast he must have driven because under normal circumstances, my house was more than an hour's drive away from that hospital.

I then learned that the personnel at the Santaquin hospital were not skilled enough to properly treat me and that they had telephoned the best-known oral surgeon in all of Utah to come down and examine me. Dr. Cray drove south to Santaquin from Provo to examine me and said, "I can certainly treat you, but I can't do it here." So he ordered another ambulance and then had me transferred to his hospital in Provo: Utah Valley Regional. There he spent nearly all night operating on me to stop the bleeding and to begin what turned out to be a very long road of healing, gradually rebuilding over years all that I had lost in only seconds.

...behold, I will tell you in your mind and in your heart, by the Holy Ghost, which shall come upon you and which shall dwell in your heart. (D&C 8:2)

CHAPTER 14
MORE UNPAVED ROADS, AND THEN...

Before I went into that first surgery, I asked Alex to please call my good friend Pauline who lived right there in Provo. He apparently did so just as I went in because he later told me that when they wheeled me out of surgery, both he and Pauline had been pacing the hospital inside and out, waiting for my surgery to end. After that five-six hours, when they finally got to see me, Pauline told me that both she and Alex burst into tears at the sight of my face. So it wasn't just my mother who didn't recognize me after the "accident." Pauline is also the one who dubbed Donald with the moniker "Stupid." It was so fitting for him; I adopted that as well.

After my mom had spent that first day with me in the hospital caring for my needs, I was settled in by the nurse for my first night after surgery. She made sure I was warm but not hot, that I was as comfortable as I could be in my hospital bed, turned off the overhead lights in my room, and left the door to my room slightly ajar. I began sliding into that drug-induced ethereal realm of no pain when I gradually became aware of quiet voices all around me. I also could hear what sounded like fabric swishing as people moved about in elaborate gowns. I was so exhausted and still in a lot of pain, but reluctantly, I opened my eyes, seeing no one. I could still hear their voices, however, and I somehow realized that they were talking about me and that they were there to tend to me through the night. My room was filled with these loving, but not visible beings! Feeling assured that I was very safe and very loved, I again closed my eyes and drifted into a very deep sleep.

My second night after surgery brought a similar experience to the first, but this time, I could distinguish only three people: my Daddy, my grandma (who died in September 1986 and was the only grandparent I ever knew), and probably the Holy Spirit or the Savior Himself. The Savior and the Holy Spirit each have the same effect in my mind and heart, so which of those two was the third being in my room is really of no importance.

Upon the time I was to be released from the hospital, Alex was planning to pick me up to give me a ride home—in the same car that only days before had a huge hole in the windshield, kind of imploded inward, just slightly right of center on the passenger's side.

March 9, 1996

I HAD NOW BEEN in the hospital for five days, and I was finally declared well enough to be released to home. They placed me in a wheelchair and took me down the elevator, where Alex was waiting for me at the hospital's front entrance to make the forty-five minute drive from the Provo hospital to my home in Magna.

About three weeks following that first hospitalization, Alex called me and wanted to take me for a ride, if only to get me out of the house. I remember dragging myself out of bed, excited to have the change of scenery from my four bedroom walls.

As I dressed and looked in the mirror, I did not recognize the face staring back at me. Though the swelling had mostly disappeared, the evidence of great trauma still remained. The drastic altering of my image made me shed a few more tears.

After we had ridden around for a while, Alex brought up the subject of the "accident." He made a statement something to the effect of, "Yeah, you were out for at least a minute; maybe two." Given our topic of conversation right before The Rock, I just couldn't let this seemingly innocent comment pass by, and I said, "Would you like to know where I was?"

Alex visibly winced, and very timidly said, "Yeah..." So I told him. I'm not sure what he was thinking while I relayed my journey, because he didn't say, but he knew that I would not lie to him.

DURING THIS INITIAL RECOVERY time, my doctor had made a partial insert of teeth (called a flipper) that I could wear while in public to avoid impolite stares. Unfortunately, at this time, I was also looking for work (again!), and the flipper helped support my self-assurance around strangers.

For one particular interview, I didn't wear my flipper because my mouth was very sore that day. The owner of the accounting office proceeded to interview me, and I could tell the exact moment that he noticed my lack of front teeth, and also my lessened enunciation (turns out you need teeth to not slur). He immediately began speaking to me as though I were less intelligent or less qualified.

After a few moments of that, I stood up suddenly and pronounced, "I am not going to waste any more of your time, or mine, because clearly, this is not a good fit for me to be employed here. But you should know that I am not a stupid person, and I don't appreciate being treated as such." I left his office wondering, What would Jesus do? Certainly not how that accountant acted! I wish I had asked him if he'd ever heard the saying, "Be nice to me; I could be your boss someday."

My dear readers, please be keenly aware of your ripple effects; they always go farther and wider than you can possibly imagine.

Around July of 1996, the friends in our "dance family" were throwing a housewarming for one of our friends who had just moved into a new apartment. Alex took me to the party, but then he acted kind of stand-offish the whole evening. Near the end of the evening, he tugged my hand and asked me to walk with him out in the courtyard away from the party. Tearily, he told me he had been hypnotized in desperation to know what really happened, and he learned that some kids were horse-playing around in the back of a light yellow, older model pickup truck; that as they drove slowly up the canyon, they were just throwing rocks and didn't mean to hurt anyone. I then shared that I'd had a dream some weeks before, which gave me the same information. He was stunned.

A couple of weeks after the party, we went dancing again, because that was a sure way to lift our spirits. Alex and I were talking while dancing, and he made a request of me. I cannot specifically remember what it was, but I do remember my response to him: "I gave you ten pounds[5] and five teeth; what more do you want?" At first, he looked a little shocked, but then he saw my mischievous grin and burst out laughing, which was my hoped-for reaction. Laughter really is wonderful medicine.

DURING THE WHOLE SUMMER of 1996, I also began to feel like dating again, since Alex had basically pulled away by this point. (On a hunch, I had done a little online snooping and learned that he too was not single; *really?* Am I a magnet for wandering men?) Two of the local sister

---

[5] My liquid diet for six weeks straight had caused the extremely fast weight loss. As a fitness professional, I DO NOT recommend strictly liquids as a healthy way to lose weight. It almost always comes back at least double.

radio stations were operating a "dating service," which was computer-based and matched people with the data in the character profiles they submitted. The two radio stations shared the computer database, and a person could enroll through either station. It was free to sign up, but the money charges came when you checked your voice messages. To this point, I had only met a lot of "toads" in search of a "prince" and was getting frustrated and discouraged. I had determined that I would check my messages just one more time because it was getting quite costly and not resulting in anything of value.

On Saturday, August 10, 1996, I listened to a message from a nice-sounding gentleman who lived in the Ogden, Utah area. At first, I was a little disheartened at the distance between our residences. But after talking for several minutes, we agreed to meet at a halfway point in Bountiful, Utah, to see the movie *Multiplicity* at the Gateway Theaters. (Fortuitous theater name? Perhaps.) That was a great choice for a first date because the movie was full of laughs.

Darrin had described himself on the phone, and when I walked up the steps of the theater, I said simply, "Is it you?" which was a line from one of my favorite movies. Unbeknownst to me, *Somewhere in Time* is also one of Darrin's favorite movies.

Our evening was very much fun, and we went for frozen yogurt afterward, to eat while we walked and talked on the grounds at the Bountiful Temple. We finally ended our date at 1:00 A.M., having made arrangements for him to attend church with me in my home ward (congregation) in Magna.

Four days later, Darrin was preparing to leave for a week-long trip to Lake Powell with one of his daughters, and his younger brother and wife. The day before he left, we were talking—as we had every day since we'd met—and he suddenly popped *the* question. I was so stunned that I couldn't/didn't answer, even though I knew what my answer would be.

You see, the whole time we were walking and talking on the temple grounds the night we met, the Spirit had been telling me, "This is the man you're going to marry," to which I argued, "No I'm not; I just met him, and I'm not even attracted to him yet." (Not quite the truth, or I wouldn't have been on that first date.)

The next morning Darrin called me to say goodbye before leaving on his trip, and he said, "You know, last night, I remember popping a question, but I don't remember getting an answer." I could only splutter, "That's because I didn't give you one. Have fun in Lake Powell; see ya next week!" *Click*. I could barely breathe.

That evening I sought out a priesthood blessing from my church leaders without telling them *why* I wanted this blessing. The following Sunday, during said blessing, I was blessed with clarity of mind that I could make the decision the Lord wanted me to make. (I'm telling you, the priesthood power is *real!*) Well, as I said, I already knew the answer. Just how to tell my mother?

But if ye will turn to the Lord with full purpose of heart, and put your trust in him, and serve him with all diligence of mind, if ye do this, he will, according to his own will and pleasure, deliver you out of bondage. (Mosiah 7:33)

CHAPTER 15
REACHING SUMMIT AFTER SUMMIT

DARRIN RICHARDS AND I were married by his bishop on November 15, 1996. We were sealed for time and all eternity exactly 2½ years later in the Bountiful Temple, shortly following my re-baptism into the Church of Jesus Christ of Latter-Day Saints. Who would have thought a computer dating service would yield such wonderful results, yet we have already celebrated more than 23 years of marriage. We also celebrate 31 grandchildren (who are definitely the cutest), eight great-grandchildren (cuter still), and singing together for years in a local community choir. (We both have sung in choirs since our junior high days.) More recently, we have become actively involved in genealogy and seeking after our ancestors. We are also ordinance workers in the Jordan River Temple of the Church. What a great privilege and blessing this has been!

JUST TO GIVE YOU an idea of my healing process, the following is a summary of the events that took place after the "accident."

Since my upper jaw had been completely shattered, it needed to be rebuilt before I could hope to support any prosthetic teeth. Nearly a year after the "accident," in late February 1997, my first bone graft was harvested from my right iliac crest (hip bone), because that is the thickest bone in the human body, providing more bone to harvest. Again, I spent five days in the hospital before I could go home. Unfortunately, in the weeks following this surgery #2, I got an infection that split open my stitches, and the bone graft subsequently died.

About two months later, my second bone graft (surgery #3) was taken from my chin, where Dr. Cray had to peel back my lower lip. He left a small dent in my chin, which is not visible, but it can be felt if you know where to touch. I also have to be careful how I rest my chin on my hands because it is still tender to a certain kind of firm touch and/or at a certain angle. This surgery was an in-office surgery, but still, I was given general anesthesia. Again, in the following weeks, it became infected, and the grafted bone died.

Surgery #4 was my third bone graft, for which the

doctor used synthetic bone. Inexplicably, this is the graft that finally "took." Praises be.

I went on to have skin graft surgery three times, all with general anesthesia, each time pulling down more skin from inside my upper lip until the doctor could pull no more without affecting my normal lip function. For the rest of my mortal life, my left side upper lip has much less space between the gums and the lip, but I've gotten used to it by now.

The oral surgeon and prosthodontist originally planned to place four implants in a row in my upper jaw after the bone grafting was finally healed enough, but apparently, I was only meant to have three implants, because my body kept rejecting the implant in one particular position. After rejecting it three times, with many tears, much disappointment, and great pain, finally, in August of 1998, it was time for them to permanently install my prosthetic. which would replace the four teeth in a row that I had lost on my upper left gum line.

Darrin took me out to eat after they placed my prosthetic, and I then learned I could not eat at my normal speed. I told him, "Be patient; I'm learning how to drive new teeth." The feeling was so weird; my new teeth felt *so big*.

During that very first surgery to stop the bleeding and stabilize my mouth, Dr. Cray also found that all of my sinuses (both right and left) had all been damaged, and he had to repair them as well. Yet more scar tissue which cannot be seen.

I endured a total of seven surgeries over a 2½ year period, including three bone grafts, three skin grafts, and replacing the oral implants that my body kept rejecting. I was instructed to take very special care of my mouth for the rest of my life, or if I didn't, they would have to hammer the prosthetic out of my mouth to replace it. My eyes went wide, and I firmly told them, "Oh no, you're not!" Just the very thought makes my mouth hurt. I brush and floss better than the best of them! I never want to go through oral surgery again if I can help it.

Now, I'm sure no one would ever think that these types of injuries would affect the entire rest of my life after they finished rebuilding my mouth. However, I can no longer take a flight comfortably (altitude is too high); I can no longer spend a day on the ski slopes (again, the altitude); I can no longer enjoy a good thunderstorm (barometer changes make me hurt because that is a change in air pressure); and we cannot go camping anyplace above 7,200 feet elevation, because I simply cannot handle the change in air pressure. I have become a good weather barometer because I will feel a rain or snow storm 1-2 days before it actually arrives. Every time the barometer changes, I hurt. It's almost like having arthritis in my mouth and face. I have pain every single day, though I try not to complain because quite frankly, nobody wants to hear it. I just try to stay busy and distracted and not focus on my pain. Part of that focus shift includes doing what I can for others just because they may need help in one way or another.

My smile is different now, and as I age, I've noticed that I am getting more wrinkles in the trauma area around my mouth than on the other side of my face. After my Lasik about fifteen years ago, my left eye took twice as long to heal as the right eye because of the previous trauma to the left side of my head and face. The scar on my lip is not very noticeable anymore, because I worked diligently to rub shark liver oil into the scar. A friend of mine suggested that I take shark liver oil gelcaps in addition to using the topical. Studies have shown that shark liver oil is a wonderful aid in healing the human body and eliminating scars because, after sharks mate, the female spends two to three weeks producing massive amounts of her liver oil to heal the wounds from the thrashing that takes place during the sharks' mating process. Thankfully, this oil works very well on humans, too. Unfortunately, it is no longer available for purchase. I will tell you that it was not a coincidence for it to have been available when I needed it most. I don't believe in coincidences, and no one will ever convince me otherwise.

He hath delivered my soul in peace from the battle that was against me, for there were many with me.

(Psalms 55:18)

EPILOGUE

For a very long time after my accident, I felt bitterness and resentment towards whoever threw The Rock at me. I resented the fact that I could no longer do the activities I had really enjoyed doing, and that I no longer recognized my own reflection in the mirror. Then in the October 2005 General Conference of the Church of Jesus Christ of Latter-Day Saints, our living prophet at the time, Gordon B. Hinckley, gave a talk on forgiveness. He spoke of a teen who decided to throw a twenty pound frozen turkey off an overpass of a freeway, hitting a woman in the face and causing her to endure more than six hours of surgery involving metal plates and other hardware to piece her face back together. (This is eerily familiar to me!) To make matters even more illogical, this teen only had the turkey because he stole a credit card and went on a just-for-kicks shopping spree.

However, the 44-year-old victim was more interested in salvaging the life of her unwitting 19-year-old assailant than in exacting any sort of revenge. She continually pestered prosecutors for information on how this teen was raised and what his life was like. Then she insisted on a plea deal for him to serve six months in the county jail and five years probation. This teen could have received up to 25 years in prison otherwise.

As I listened intently to President Hinckley relate this story, the tears began streaming, and I realized that I needed to let my pain and frustration and bitterness go to God. As promised for all of our life experiences, we will never feel or experience anything that our Savior has not already experienced or felt. He took the pain of everything for us if we would just accept Him as our Savior and try to emulate His life through our own lives.

I determined at that very moment that I would no longer harbor bitterness and/or resentment for my assailant(s). I testify with all of my being that my life has since improved. I know my Savior lives and loves me, and He is involved in every detail of my life, no matter how small, because of His love for me. I only need to invite Him in every day.

I have also subsequently released my bitterness towards "Stupid" for all the emotional trauma he brought into my life. I do not wish him any ill will, but he is not a safe person for me. In retrospect, that whole relationship taught me how to recognize others who are not safe persons for me, and while I would never be impolite or mean to any of them, I also don't go out of my way to associate with them anymore. It's just better that way.

I hereby invite each of my readers to take the same steps in your own life, live like the Savior lived, and invite Him into your life. He will not let you down! I so testify in the name of Jesus Christ.

WORD PHOTOGRAPHY

*Like physicians view an X-ray
'Ere they treat a fractured bone,
And the key step for new buildings
Is to lay the cornerstone;
There's a person in the courtroom
Who rarely speaks a word
But without this person present
Testimony won't be heard.
The reporter is the player
Through whom things will come to light
For the jury reads the records
While deciding what is right.*

*As an infant needs its mother
Or the sunshine feeds the trees,
Reporters fill a vital role, and
Help our system run with ease.
Trial Pictures aren't complete without
The written "photograph", for
No memory captures all things
Spoken in a man's behalf.
So reporters train their minds and hands
For writing every word;
Thus the jury will be able to
Review what they have heard.*

How our system would be crippled
If no one took the time
To teach reporters skills they need
In recording every line.
Attorneys, jurors, judges too
Rely on the accuracy
Of a wise reporter's records
To decide what "fate" will be.
Justice in a courtroom can't
Proceed without court files,
So we'd best continue training
And preserve our freedom style.

10/14/91©

www.ingramcontent.com/pod-product-compliance
Lightning Source LLC
Chambersburg PA
CBHW031117080526
44587CB00011B/1012